Richard D Harm
7445 Boulder Lake Rd
Duluth MN 55803

PSE Mach Flite 4R

* Unisystem - Quiver & site
* TM Hunter Overdraw
* XX75 Easton
  - 2213 or - 2018 } 26" for 31" draw.
* 110 gr. blades.

NORTHERN PIKE!

by
Tom Zenanko

Artwork by Buzz Buczynski, Brookston, Minn.
Cover and Inside Photos by Author

Tom Zenanko Outdoors

ISBN 0-9610296-1-7

NORTHERN PIKE!

TABLE OF CONTENTS

This book is dedicated to the little boy in all of us who would rather go fishing than work

INTRODUCTION

A few years ago on a cold January morning I received a call from a large sporting goods store in southern Minnesota. The store manager was interested in offering a fishing seminar in March and was wondering if my schedule was booked for that month. To his disappointment only a Monday evening was still available for the entire month. If he planned on having a fishing seminar, then this was the only day left. With some hesitation, he agreed and we began to work on some of the details. I had been in his town the previous year, to do a walleye fishing seminar, and he thought it wouldn't be a bad idea to change the seminar to something new. Without a second of hesitation I recommended a program on northern pike fishing. "Do people actually want to know how to catch northerns?" the shop manager questioned. "People around here don't need any help with catching those things, they catch them easy enough already."

I mentioned to him that the pike is loved by millions and how a program like this in Minnesota, where the pike is almost as popular as the walleye would be of great interest.

On a rainy Monday night in March, over a thousand people jammed the auditorium at the local high school. While the crowds were streaming in the door, the shop manager was bubbling with excitement. "I had no idea this many people really wanted to know about northern pike fishing."

After the program, comments from the fishermen attending the program had shown me the need to get more information to the public about this great fish. "Many of my friends think fishing for northern pike is as simple as fishing for panfish," commented one angler heading out the door. "I sure wish my buddies would have come to the program, they would think twice before razzing me again."

An informal survey done with fliers distributed to random audiences, revealed that the biggest reason people dislike pike is because of their "Y" bones. The majority of anglers still fish to bring something home, and the bones in a northern pike make the fillets difficult to eat. Although the procedure to remove the extra bones in a northern is very simple, the process is not commonly known.

Even the knowledge of safe handling and releasing of pike, can take a lot of effort to find. It has taken years of research to uncover many of the new tips and secrets found in this book. Pike fishing methods have been very traditional and could very well be the reason pike fishing has remained so popular.

Many of the more practical kinds of things, like sharpening a hook properly and the correct methods for netting a pike, can be important to all anglers. Every year I cringe when someone tells me of the guy from "down south," who sticks his thumb in the mouth of a northern pike to land it and ends up with fifteen stitches in his hand.

Pike fishing has a surprising amount of old wives tales, such as a reason for poor pike action would be the northern pike having sore teeth. Anglers need to know more about this great sport fish and it was time for a comprehensive book to help both the expert and amateur alike. "Northern Pike!" was written with no double talk or fancy words to make the fisherman feel they have to re-learn what they already know about fishing. Understanding pike and pike fishing from a new perspective is something every reader will get from this book.

Never has there been a fish so well loved, but yet so misunderstood as the northern pike. A fish who has been loved by royalty and the common man for centuries. Pike anglers have always been the more "bread and butter" type of angler. Even today's more sophisticated anglers are just now realizing how special the northern pike really is as a sportfish and as a part of the balance of nature.

CHAPTER ONE

The Folklore of Pike Fishing

The wind blew briskly from the west as a thunderstorm was forming just above the horizon. A youngster of eight carefully climbed into an old wooden boat attached to a dock, which shook and flexed with the weight of the young lad. The guide on this late summer fishing trip was a seasoned resort owner on a central Minnesota lake. His weathered face showed years of experience and the young angler looked to him as if he were the president of the United States. Old Bill had taken the youngster to a private or "secret lake" surrounded by woods. The night before the wide eyed boy simply begged to go fishing with Old Bill after he reminisced about "Betsy" a northern pike so large no man had ever tamed her. The story was told very convincingly by the resort owner in a quiet and almost whispered tone so as no one else could hear.

"Betsy first grabbed my spoon about eight years ago while I was out duck hunting. The ducks weren't flying, so I decided to see if there were any fish in this small lake. You see, no one can get to the lake but me, because it's five miles from the nearest road. My tractor is the only way to get to the lake. Old Betsy hit my one and only spoon after about two casts and tore every foot of line off my reel and was gone! I went right back to the same spot a day later and hooked her again, but this time I had plenty of line. She still had my other spoon in her mouth! I figure she was at least thirty pounds, but before I could club her with my oar, the line broke and she was gone again. A year later two of my fishing buddies had her on, but again she broke off. I've taken a number of my guests to Betsy's lake. One even had her in the net before she broke the line AND the net. The guy told me the northern pike he hooked had a mouth full of lures, so I knew it was Betsy. Come to think of it, it was about this time last year when a young lad of your age was pulled right into the lake before letting go of his rod and reel!"

"Gee," was all the trembling lad could say. "Do you think maybe, just maybe, we could fish that lake?" Inquired the timid lad, who would have easily sold his new bike by this time for a chance at fishing for Betsy.

As the two anglers climbed into the old wooden boat, Bill glanced up at the clouds, "We've only got about an hour before that storm gets here, so we'll go right to the area Betsy likes best and start trolling." By this time the young boy was so excited he knocked his tackle box off the seat and it's contents fell all over the bottom of the boat.

Using a stout steel rod his father gave him to use for the trip and twenty pound braided line on a bait casting reel, the stage was set. Old Bill reached into his metal tackle box and pulled out a very large black and white spoon and secured it to the boy's line with a hard pull to make sure everything was secure.

As they began trolling, Bill pointed out how to handle the big pike should she hit. He described some of her secrets for catching fishermen off guard and breaking the line. The young student absorbed as much as he could over the loud roar of the air-cooled outboard, which powered the boat.

Suddenly the lad's rod jerked, but the weight just seemed to hang on the line like a weed. " I'm snagged ," suggested the annoyed angler, but Bill was not so easily fooled. He began to shout directions and kept getting more and more excited, but the young fisherman was unaware of what was about to happen.

"Boy, I sure must have caught a pile of weeds, why didn't you get hung up too? Hey, this isn't a weed, it's..it's . . . pulling back and . . . and I can't hold it! Help!,Help!" Unfamiliar with the reel his father gave him, the only way he knew to relieve the pressure on the line was to hit the free spool button. By this time, the young lad was totally unaware of the commands Bill was shouting at the top of his lungs and seemed frozen with fright. Without a second thought the free spool bottom was pushed and the error in that method of fighting a fish would forever be etched in the mind of the inexperienced angler.

For at that moment a tangle of line spun wildly around the reel's spool creating a mess. By this time the fish had turned and was making a power dive under the boat, the steel rod banged the gunnel of the wooden boat as the helpless angler held on with all his strength. Then, the steel rod bounced upward and straightened out. The line had been broken and with it the boy's heart.

Stunned from shock, nothing was said until tears rolled down his cheeks and a loud cry of disappointment was heard all across the small lake.

This is a story from the author's past, and for northern pike anglers all across the country, this kind of lore is what keeps anglers coming back for more. In Europe the "pike" is surrounded with mystery and intrigue. Esox Lucious is the scientific name for the northern pike. Pike is a name originating in the Anglo Saxon period when a pike was a spear like slashing weapon used in battle during the middle ages. In those days, pike organs were used to cure pleurisy, ashes of burned pike were used on wounds, and pike bones guarded against witchcraft.

In French Victorian times, the northern pike were affectionately called "jacks." This accounts for why the French Canadians today call pike "jackfish." Here in the United States, the pike has been given a wide variety of nicknames like snakes, toothies, hammerhandles, and slime.

The most commonly used name is "northern pike," but even this name is not widely accepted. In Europe and many other regions of the world, just the name "pike" is used.

The reason "northern" was added to the name pike in the United States, dates back to the turn of the century. The Great Northern Railroads carried people and equipment to remote regions of Minnesota and Wisconsin. The trains would often stop near a lake, where the workers and passengers were given a chance to try their luck. The results of this wilderness style of fishing spread rapidly and before long, anglers would travel from all over the country to catch some of the "Great Northern Pike." Over the years, the "Great" was left off leaving the name we commonly use today.

The northern pike as we now call it has been around a long time and since its range is global in nature, fish stories from around the world have drew the interest of many famous anglers. Izaak Walton once wrote about the pike as "choicely good: Too good for any but anglers and honest men."

This leads us to the story of the famous "Emperor's Pike," which was said to have been stocked in a lake by Emperor Fredrick II in 1230. The fish was eventually taken from the lake in 1497, 267 years after it was stocked and it still had a brass ring in its mouth that the Emperor had attached! The pike weighed 350 pounds and was nineteen feet long! The story does not end here, the skeleton of the fish was preserved in the Mannheim Cathedral. After many years of being on exhibit, a naturalist examined the skeleton and found it had too many vertebrae and was declared a hoax!

One very interesting bit of folklore actually stems from some real-life occurrences with northern pike. One such case begins by knowing that the eagle is one of the true enemies of the pike. Pike like to sun themselves just below the water's surface and eagles love to swoop down and grab them. On one such occasion, an eagle tried to grab a pike that was much too large for it to lift out of the water, but eagle talons grab so firmly they cannot be released. This is exactly what had happened once and the eagle was drowned by the big pike. For years, the local residents thought the lake was haunted by what they called a Sjo-troll. The Sjo-troll was said to have horns of an elk and was often seen moving very rapidly just below the surface. One brave soul by the name of Lekander, shot the creature. It was found to be a huge pike with the bones of the eagle still attached to his back!

There are countless stories about big pike attacking people, horses, mules, dogs and outboard motors, all of them seem to

Stories of gigantic pike have tickled the imagination of anglers for centuries.

be told or written about with a smile and I have no warnings to give about such interesting possibilities. They are all meant to be light hearted and exciting, which is the way I feel life and fishing should be.

CHAPTER TWO

The Life of a Northern Pike

The natural range of the pike family is global in nature and has the widest distribution range of any freshwater fish. There are several popular fish which are all part of the "Esox" or pike family.

The muskellunge or muskie (Esox Masquinongy), can grow to reach eighty pounds and is the largest growing member of the pike group.

The second largest member of the pike family is a natural cross between a northern pike and muskie. This hybrid cross is called a tiger muskie.

The northern pike or just plain "pike," (Esox Lucious) is the third largest and the most abundant of all the esox family with the largest taken on hook and line weighing nearly 56 pounds.

Silver pike are a rare mutant breed of pike found in isolated regions where the northern pike is abundant. Thought to be another hybrid cross between a muskie and northern pike, this theory was dismissed when studies showed silver pike had their own unique spawning cycle later than northern pike but before the muskie, and mate successfully with other silver pike.

The Eastern regions of the United States hold the largest populations of "pickerel." This group is physically the smallest of all the pikes growing to not much more than six pounds. The Chain Pickerel (Esox Niger), Redfin Pickerel (esox Americanus) and the Grass Pickerel (Esox Americanus Vermiculatus). In a natural setting where two or more of these pickerel are found, it is common to have a hybrid cross which can make identification difficult at times.

One member of the pike family not common in the United States is the Amur pike (Esox Reicherti) which grows as large as the northern pike is often found in the USSR.

Each of the members of the pike family have their own unique tale to tell, especially the muskie. Since a muskie grows to extremely large sizes in the United States they steal much of the glory away from the northern pike. Literally hundreds of books and stories have been written about the elusive muskie.

Since this book deals with just the northern pike, it unveils things not commonly known about pike. In popularity the northern is one of the most respected gamefish world-wide. We will soon discover how difficult life is for the pike, but how they continue to bounce back.

Early pike anglers often referred to the pike as the "water wolf" and in many cases, the comparison is well given because of it's willingness to attack almost anything. The northern is really a top of the line predator who can eat almost anything. If conditions make feeding difficult, northern pike can cut food consumption down to relatively nothing and still live. To the young pike, countless pitfalls await, not to mention the odds it must overcome to hatch in the first place.

A four pound female pike can lay as many as 50,000 eggs! If mother nature is willing and it is not too cold, too hot, too dry or too wet. Two to eight percent of the eggs will hatch if severe conditions do not kill the eggs. Northern pike like to spawn in flooded vegetation and marshes off the main lake or river which are often heavily populated with predatory creatures. Male and female pike will migrate up rivers or creeks as the ice leaves the lake. Spawning is done in daylight as a male northern softly bumps and rubs the sides of the larger female. When the moment is right the eggs and milk are released and permitted to randomly fall into the submerged vegetation.

Depending greatly on water temperature, the eggs hatch within two weeks and the young pike will live off the original egg sack for about ten days before needing to feed on various microscopic organisms. At this time insects, birds, perch and other adult pike feed on the tiny offspring.

As the fry grow, they consume great amounts of food. If the supply of food is cut off for even a short period, the small pike feed on other pike!

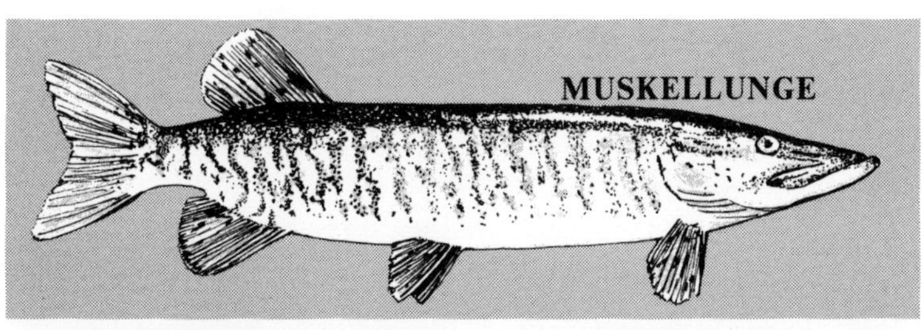

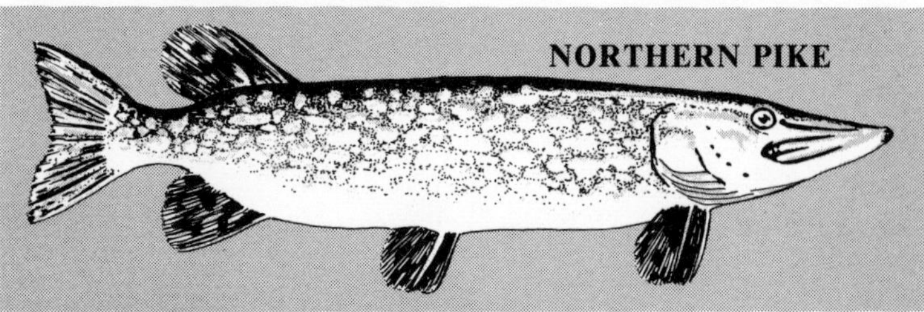

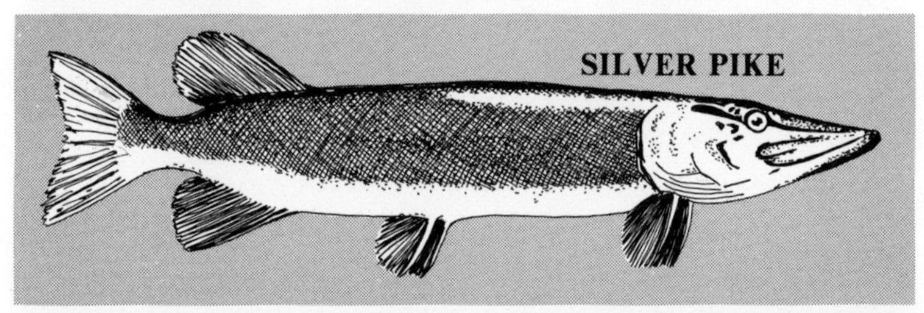

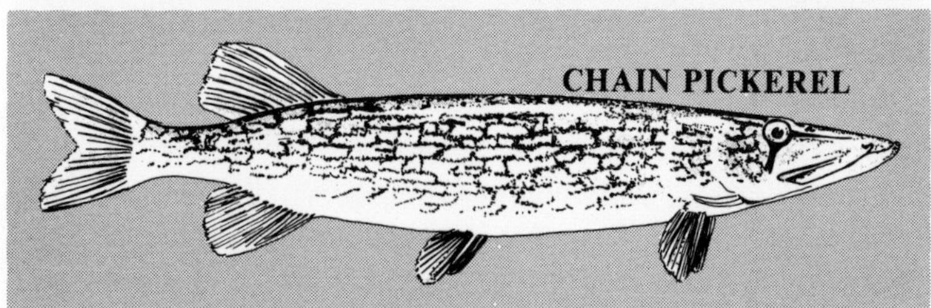

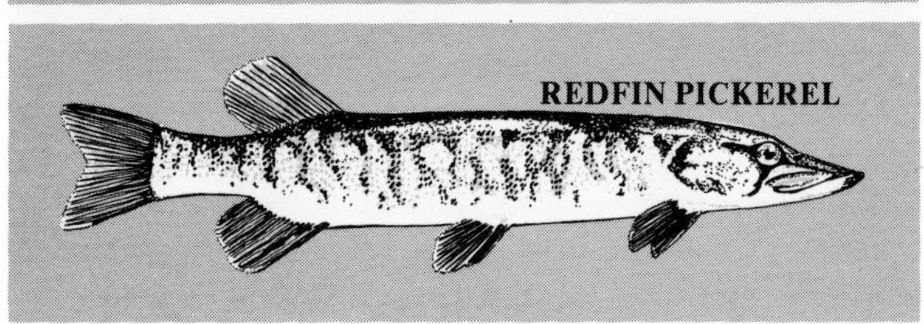

Above are five members of the Esox family. Although body shapes are similar, each member has its own individual life style.

GLOBAL DISTRIBUTIO

Water temperature seems to be a major factor in the rate of time it takes both the male and female pike to reach maturity.

A female can be ready to spawn in four years and a male in three. This growth pattern will vary greatly because in nature, there are countless combinations of factors that can control fish growth and development. It would be rash to make bold statements on why some lakes have big northern pike while others have only hammer handles without extensive research.

One interesting thing to note about the pike is the way it thrives in cold water. A unique fact that is note worthy is contrary to the majority of other fishes found in the colder regions of the continent. The northern pike is capable of growth in both summer **AND** winter! This factor supports some interesting possibilities for fish location. In some Southern regions where pike were introduced, a newborn pike can grow to 17 inches in the first year! While in the Northwest Territories of Canada,

OF NORTHERN PIKE

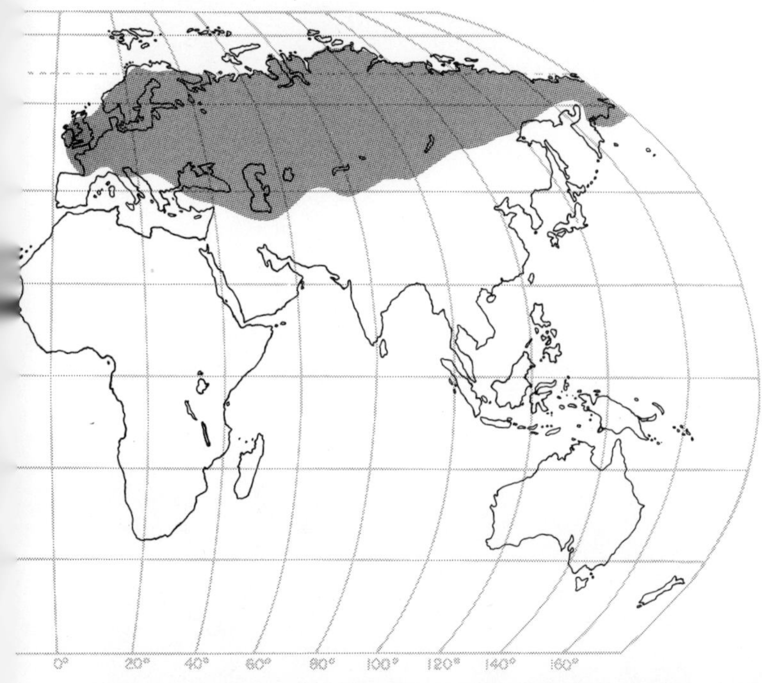

a northern pike may only grow three inches during the same period of time. The life span of the Southern pike is shorter than one living in extremely cold regions. A life span of 12 to 15 years is average for most pike, with the maximum life of about twenty years.

Immature pike have different color markings than their parents and this changing of color patterns can make identification of one and two year old pike rather confusing. In most cases, the color pattern of stripes or bars will remain present until they reach maturity.

Many factors tend to control the adult pikes color pattern. On any given lake, pike will vary in color from a bright green to an almost pale yellow. Some experts believe the color of a pike is hereditary, while others are confident water quality and forage determine pike coloration. No clear cut answer has been found yet, but the exterior color of a freshly caught pike

These two pike were taken not more than ten minutes apart. Note the obvious color differences in the two fish. The various color shades of pike can range from dark green to almost silver.

has no bearing on the eating quality of the fish.

As fry, the male pike grow faster than the females during the first year. This could possibly be one of natures safety valves for thinning out the amount of egg laying females if the lakes and rivers they are spawning in are unsuited for more pike. The larger male fry will rapidly begin feeding on the smaller females if food is not abundant. After the first year, the rate of growth for the females begins to exceed the male. This increased rate of growth will continue until they are nearing the end of their life span. A female pike's total body weight may be 25 pounds in fourteen years, but at sixteen, that same fish may only weigh 18 pounds! Once pike reach their maximum size, which is determined greatly on availability of food, the pike just stop growing. In some lakes they may top out at fifteen pounds, while other lakes are suited to raise pike up to thirty pounds. This is also true of male pike, but a male never reaches more than ten pounds even with the most ideal conditions.

The long streamline bodies of the adult pike can vary in proportion. In many of the remote Canadian lakes, northern pike are commonly found to have large heads and thin bodies. Many believe that pike coming from lakes without an abundant food supply tend to feed more sparingly and on larger forms of food.

When the food supply runs low, northern pike will feed on almost anything they can get their jaws around, and that even includes other northern pike!

Over the years, the head of the pike seems to grow, while the body remains the same. Some anglers claim they can identify the body shape of a pike right down to a particular lake. This of course can not be done with any kind of certainty, but pike from different lake types tend to develope their body proportions in a similar way.

A healthy, well fed pike population finds the head on a northern pike small and the bodies very thick and broad. These kinds of pike shapes are commonly found in the southern regions of where pike thrive.

Mature female pike are always larger than males of the same age. This is an interesting subject which could apply to many other species. In the world of fish, the female is almost always the larger of the two. One intriguing theory was examined in "Pike and the Pike Angler" by Fred Buller, one of England's finest anglers. Mr. Buller pointed to the actual spawning ritual as the answer. During the act of spawning, the pike use an eye-to-eye method of orientation. When pike of equal size try to mate, the males milt suspends in the water like a cloud **BEHIND** both pike, so there is no way the sinking eggs can get fertilized before they settle to the bottom. The water currents created as the pike swim and mate at the same time would keep the males milt above and behind the eggs. A smaller pike when matched eye-to-eye with a larger female will create a cloud of milt for the eggs to pass through instead of falling below. As a result, over the years a selective breeding process has taken place where shorter bodied males became more successful parents.

This theory is very logical and could very well be the reason why male pike do not grow as large as females. Biologist tell us it is rare to find a male pike exceeding nine pounds. Although stories may be told about anglers who have caught twenty pound male pike, in nearly all cases the assumption was made from an outward observation or when a female's ovary had failed to develop completely, then assuming it to be a male. Only a trained eye can tell for sure the sex of a pike with 100% accuracy, and this is especially true of immature pike.

From a fisherman's standpoint, male pike tend to fight much harder and with more determination than females do for fish of the same size. This has been noted many times with fish biol-

When anglers catch a fine stringer of pike like this, it is a sure bet that every pike shown here is a female.

ogists use for studies. I can remember one pike that almost took the rod right out of my hand! While fishing a lake in southern Minnesota I had made a comment to my fishing partner after landing a beautiful ten pound pike that it sure was not much of a battle. On the next cast I hooked another pike that stretched my line to the breaking point before the rod tip could be dropped into the water to follow the fish and loosen the pressure on the line as the reel's drag could be re-set. Time was not on my side as the unseen torpedo raced under the boat with me up to my elbows in water. Finally, the fish turned and one of the truly best fights I can remember continued. When all was said and done, only a four pound male northern pike was netted, but what a wildcat!

Disease

Fish in general, can all fall victim to many different forms of disease and the northern pike is no exception. One of the most common is the black spot disease which covers the skin of small northern pike. This disease is made when free swimming cereariae penetrate the skin and a black spot develops caused by a trematodes. Little is known about how this form of parasite decides where to strike. It appears only smaller pike are effected and it does seem to hinder the growth rates of fish which are infected. For some reason, adult fish very seldom contract the disease. It poses no health problem for humans if the skin is removed while cleaning and the meat is cooked properly.

Unsightly tumor like growths can be found on the sides of large pike. This is of no concern to the angler as long as the tumor-like tissue is cut off, but it can be harmful to other pike in the lake. Rather than throwing the fish back, it would be wise to keep it so other pike will not be contaminated by this contagious growth.

Rare cases of tape worm, different kinds of fungi, leeches and even lampreys can be found in or on northern pike at times. Although these diseases and parasites mentioned above are rarely if ever harmful to humans, the proper cleaning and preparing of the fillets will insure safe consumption with no side affects.

Feeding Habits

Throughout the ages, the northern pike has been said to eat everything from ducks, swans, muskrats, children's toys and even humans! The "never turn down a meal" attitude of the pike has set the stage for some very colorful stories.

Small northern pike have an appetite that is almost unstoppable. As they grow older, the adult northern feed more sparingly. As the pike grows, it becomes capable of feeding on a larger and larger variety of fish, and now animals.

The northern pike relies on three basic senses to feed. Eyesight is by far one of the most important senses to the pike. The northern possess a unique eye among fish in that it can absorb great amounts of sunlight without pain or discomfort. The pike is then free to swim below the surface on a bright sunny day without a care. Many believe pike feed exclusively by sight, but this has been proven false. Of the senses, sight is the single most important sense for many pike. Anglers will find the daylight hours the best time for fishing.

In Europe, more and more anglers are fishing successfully for pike during the hours of darkness. Having personally taken several large northern pike at night myself over the years, I find it depends greatly on the type of lake or river to be fished as to how active the pike will be during the night. Water clarity does seem to have a bearing on night-time pike activity. the dirty or heavily stained lakes tend to have more night time feeding activity than lakes which are gin clear. Northern pike want to be the most productive predators possible when they are hungry, so they will feed when the advantage to strike is in their favor. Bright sunlight that is dreaded by other predatory fish can be easily tolerated by pike, so they are much more willing to feed at mid-day.

At night or in lakes with low visibility, northern pike tend to rely more on scent and sound to find their prey. Bait fishing methods in pike fishing are effective in such lakes and over the

Some of the most bizarre tales of pike feeding activity have entertained anglers for hundreds of years.

course of many years, anglers on a local basis seem to know which lakes can be successfully fished at night. A greater understanding of artificial lures that create the most noise and vibration in the water would be an excellent choice in lakes where pike have a rough time visually seeing the lure.

Night fishing for northerns can produce some outstanding results. More and more anglers are finding some lakes are actually better for the large northern after dark. At first pike were thought to be daytime feeders only, but fishermen are having some note worthy success after sunset.

A common occurence anglers run into while fishing pike with artificial lures is the pike's rather near sightedness. On more than one occasion a pike would strike at a lure and miss it time after time. One pike over shot the lure by four feet and cut the fishing line a foot above the leader! Often when pike are visually spotting it's prey, it is wise to use a steady retrieve so the northern can plan a more successful attack. Once the large duck like jaws of the pike is open, the fish cannot see the lure that maybe only inches away! It is the habit of pike to make a quick grabbing motion to gain control of the lure, but often misses! How aggressively the pike are feeding by sight can often be determined by just how many swirls behind the bait occur before actually hooking a fish! Fishermen might think that after watching a pike miss a slow moving lure several times a northern pike must have a rough time of catching other fish, but the pike is capable of using other senses to feed as well.

The sense of smell given to the pike is very well developed, but many anglers fail to take advantage of this well developed sense and use it to their advantage. This book will discuss at length the methods of fishing with scent appealing baits that can open the door to a whole new frontier to pike fishing. Northern pike will not work any harder than they absolutely have to feed. If this means feeding on dead or dying fish on the bottom of a lake, so be it!

Sound is the third major sense the pike use for feeding. This is especially true in stained or dirty water lakes where visibility is limited. Lures that have large spinners often are used by anglers who fish dirty water lakes and many of those secrets for better success will be pointed out in later chapters.

To survive, the northern pike can adapt very well to nearly any body of water thus showing no preference for what it can or cannot digest in its stomach. The unique way a pike feeds on prey almost half its size is unique among fish. If for example: a pike grabs a large sucker minnow weighing three pounds, but the pike only weighs six pounds. The needle sharp teeth of the pike can hold its prey in a death grip because the inward slant given to the teeth will permit only the inward movement of the sucker. The elastic stomach sack of the northern pike can stretch to hugh proportions as the sucker is drawn into it head first. The throat of the pike tightens around whatever portion of the sucker that does not fit into the stomach to prevent the pike from actually drowning by swallowing unwanted amounts of water. Meanwhile, the strong digestive fluids of the pike quickly dissolve the sucker. When enough room has been made in the stomach, the pike makes another gulp and this process is repeated until all of the sucker has been swallowed.

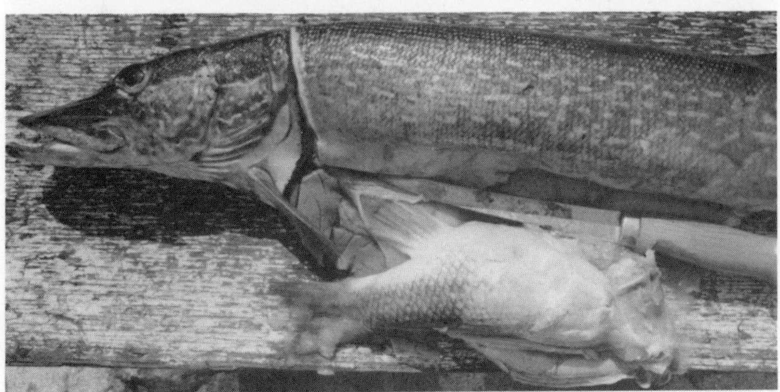

It is amazing how a northern can swallow a baitfish nearly half its size.On some lakes where food is scarce, pike learn quickly to feed whenever they can. This eight pound pike still had part of a three pound white sucker in her stomach when she hit a spoon ten inches long!

Some experiments done in Germany with northern pike seem to indicate that pike prefer prey that are 10 to 15 percent of its body weight! When fishermen say "big fish, big bait," they may be right.

Adult Pike

The adult northern pike is not as blood thirsty as its younger brothers and sisters. Adult pike like to spend a great deal of their time resting in deeper water haunts. A series of growth studies have been conducted along with their relationship to

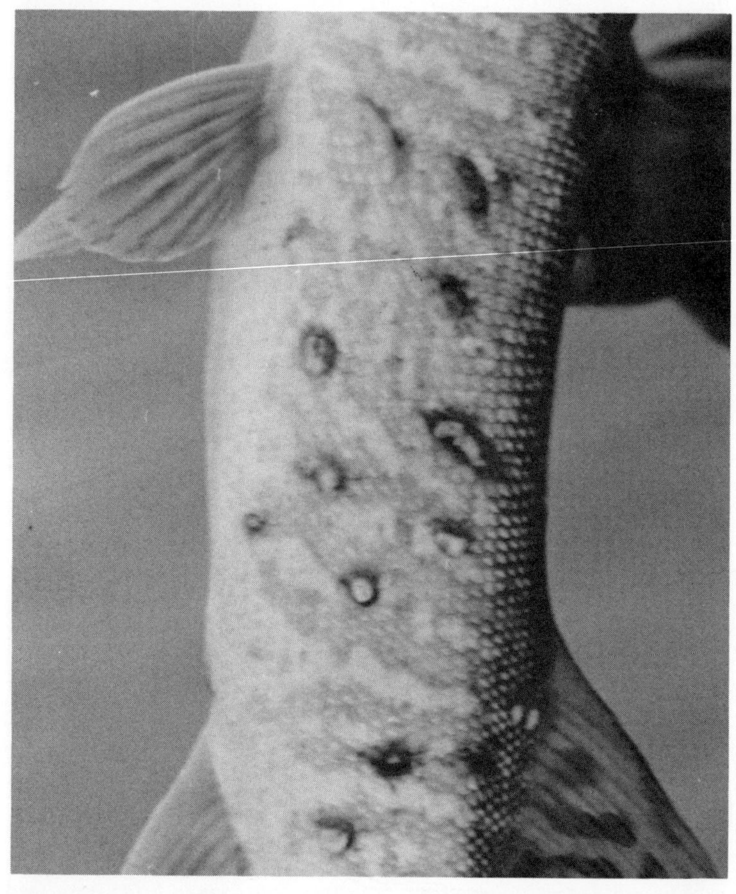

Believe it or not, this four pound pike was caught after it was attacked by another northern pike. The tooth marks on both sides of the pike spanned thirteen inches!

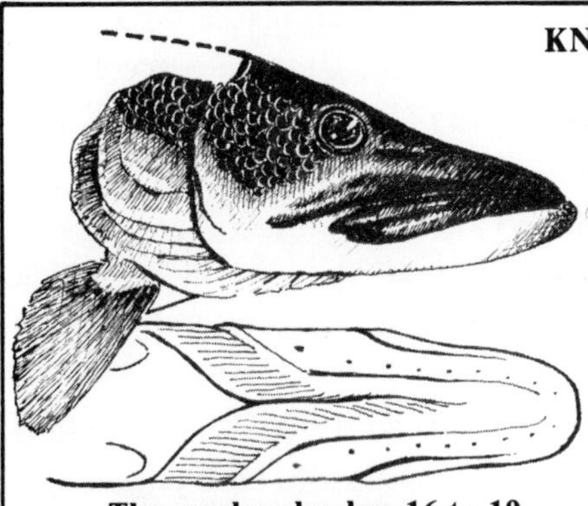

KNOW THE DIFFERENCE:

The musky has scales down the upper half of the cheeks and gills; the lower half is unscaled.
The musky has from 14 to 17 sensory pores located under the jaw.

MUSKY

The musky also has 16 to 19 bony rays in the gills.

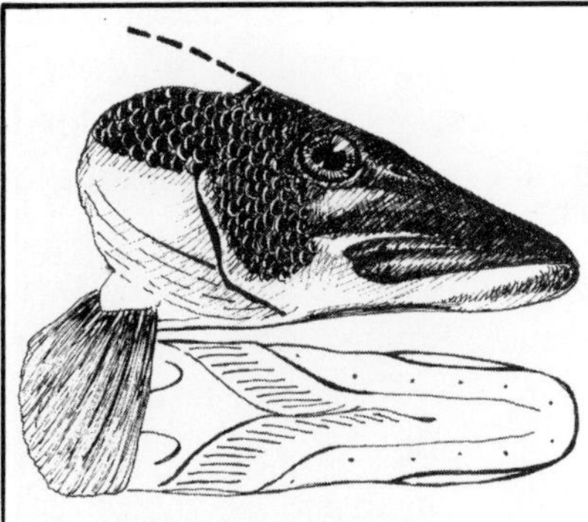

KNOW THE DIFFERENCE:
The northern pike has scaled covered cheeks but only half-scaled gill coverings.
The northern pike has 10 sensory pore openings.

NORTHERN PIKE

The northern pike has 14 bony rays in the gills.

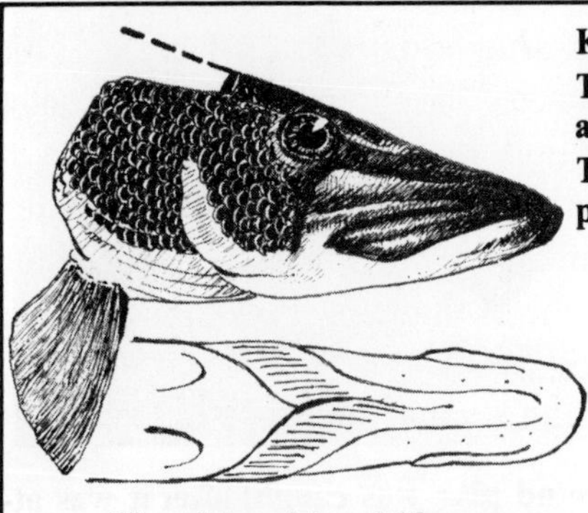

KNOW THE DIFFERENCE:
The pickerel has both cheeks and gill coverings fully scaled.
The pickerel has only 8 sensory pore openings.

PICKEREL

The pickerel has 16 bony rays in the gills.

feeding activity and some very interesting results have shown up which would seem to directly affect angling success.

Since fish are cold blooded, it is logical to assume the warmer the water, the more active they become and the more food they will need to survive. Numerous studies show the growth periods of the northern pike do not occur when the weather is the hottest. The big pike actually seem to lay dormant in the heat and feed very little.

This may shock many who believed for years that if a good angler was out on a lake, they would have no problem catching all the big pike they wanted. Since the pike just seemed to disappear, many anglers believe the theory that the big pike just move to a different area on a lake, like to deep water and seek out new types of food fish. The fact that the pike have relocated out in deep water in some lakes is very likely, but the point is that pike are not feeding with the same constant hunger they once had as youngsters.

It must be stated that we are talking about **BIG** northern pike, ones in excess of ten pounds. Smaller pike will continue to feed heavily at all times and never seem to turn down a chance at a morsel of food.

With this knowledge of big pike growth and feeding activity, when would be the best time to be out on the water? Light levels and not temperature were shown in studies to be more important in getting the bigger fish moving and feeding again. March is a peak month for the big females to feed and so is the end of August to early September. This is also the prime months during the year when the majority of the big pike are taken as well. The northern pike feeding frenzy will last only about ten days. Anglers cashing in on this truly prime time to be on the water will hook and land some of the largest pike the lake has to offer.

The million dollar question would then be: Were the big northern always in the same area and just would not bite, or are they just moving into the area from some other deep water holding area? Why only now, when the days become noticeably shorter and the air cooler do the big pike come back to life? For these questions there are no clear cut answers, but in nature many other fish seem to live and feed better at preferred water

Large pike often travel in groups of two. Anglers who take one large pike from an area should be ready for more action.Pike really do not school like walleyes, but packs of big northerns often patrol certain areas.

temperatures. It is not unreasonable to believe that mature northern pike have the same basic desire to seek out a comfortable temperature as other fish.

Mature pike like to travel in loose groups and tend to be individuals in the way they move about in a lake. To say that pike actually school like walleyes would be wrong. Pike prefer feeding in pairs or maybe in groups up to eight. The largest pike tend to control an area in groups of two. Anglers will often find two large fish of almost identical size working the same sunken island or point.

Only recently with the advent of radio tracking systems have we gotten any kind of feel for where and how the pike moves about in a lake. Some northern pike move around almost constantly, while others prefer to stay within casting distance of the same area all season. The pike who did move about would show a rather strange habit of following the same circular course on a lake and visit the same spots each time around. This pattern would continue both summer **AND** winter in a nine-day cycle! This is only the results of one particular study because lake size and configuration all play a part in the distances and ways big pike travel. Pike, who like to move about, can easily cover a mile of water in a day, while others will prefer to move only a few yards.

The results of studies offer some very intriguing facts that are nice to know, but what will it do for you in increasing your success as an angler? Veteran guide and pike angler, Mike McClelland, from Pierre, South Dakota, once compared fishing to the building of a brick wall. Every piece of information you learn in fishing is another brick, and the only way to make a good wall is with many bricks!

Northern Pike Management

Public acceptance of pike in the United States has seen many different phases, from total rejection and dislike, to becoming one of the most popular fish in the country!

The first records of pike management date back to the eleventh century in Bohemia where farm ponds were used to breed this royal fish. For centuries the northern pike was raised in private ponds in Europe and was considered to be a very stylish item to own. Many of the moats that surrounded castles were heavily stocked with pike to help protect the castle!

In the United States, the first management problem given to the fish and game departments was how to get rid of the pike.

Public pressure from lake shore owners succeeded in removing thousands of pounds of northern pike from lakes in the upper Midwest so the more desirable species would have a chance to flourish!

This short sightedness of the early sportsmen spelled doom for pike. Many of the other more desirable species suddenly became overly abundant and stunted in size as they were never thinned out and permitted to grow. Today, the northern pike is used heavily by the Fish and Game Departments as a tool for better management on lakes. This natural way of correcting a predator-VS-prey imbalance not only solves the problem of stunted fish populations, but also offers another great fishing opportunity for anglers.

Pike are simply too valuable a resource to waist needlessly. Anglers should take the time to carefully release their fish to fight again another day.

COMMON FOOD FISH FOR NORTHERN PIKE

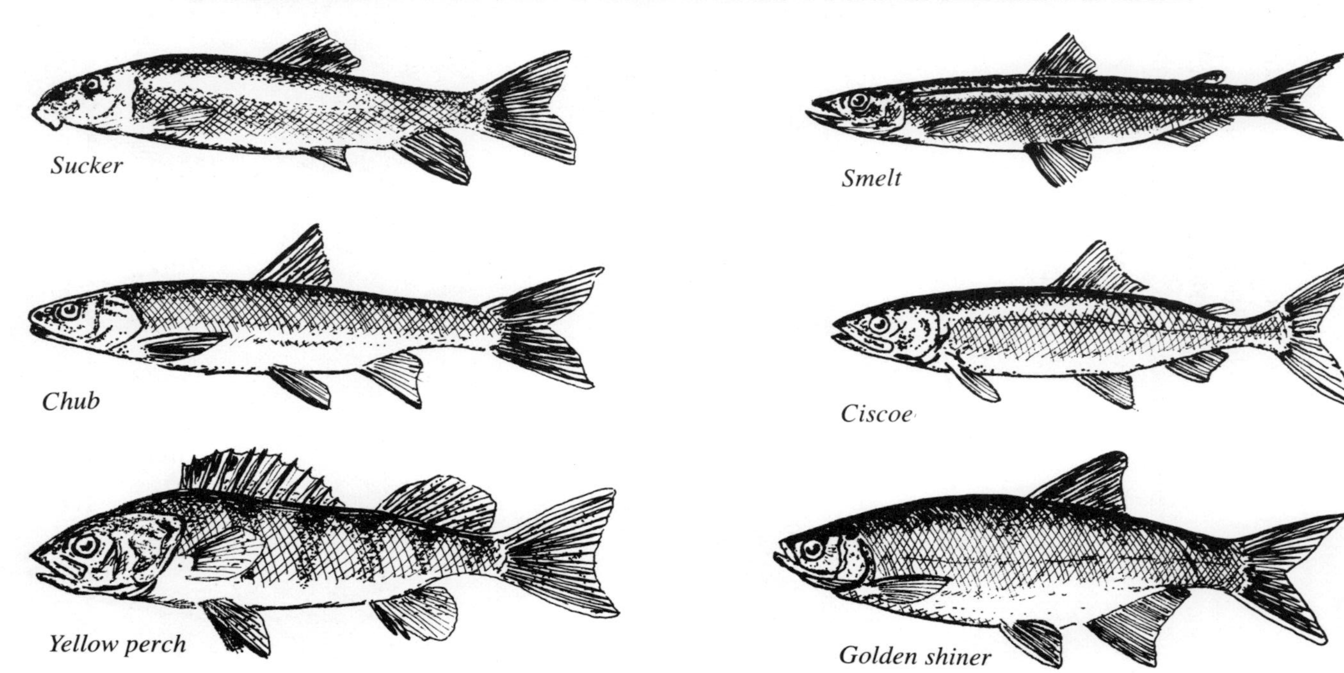

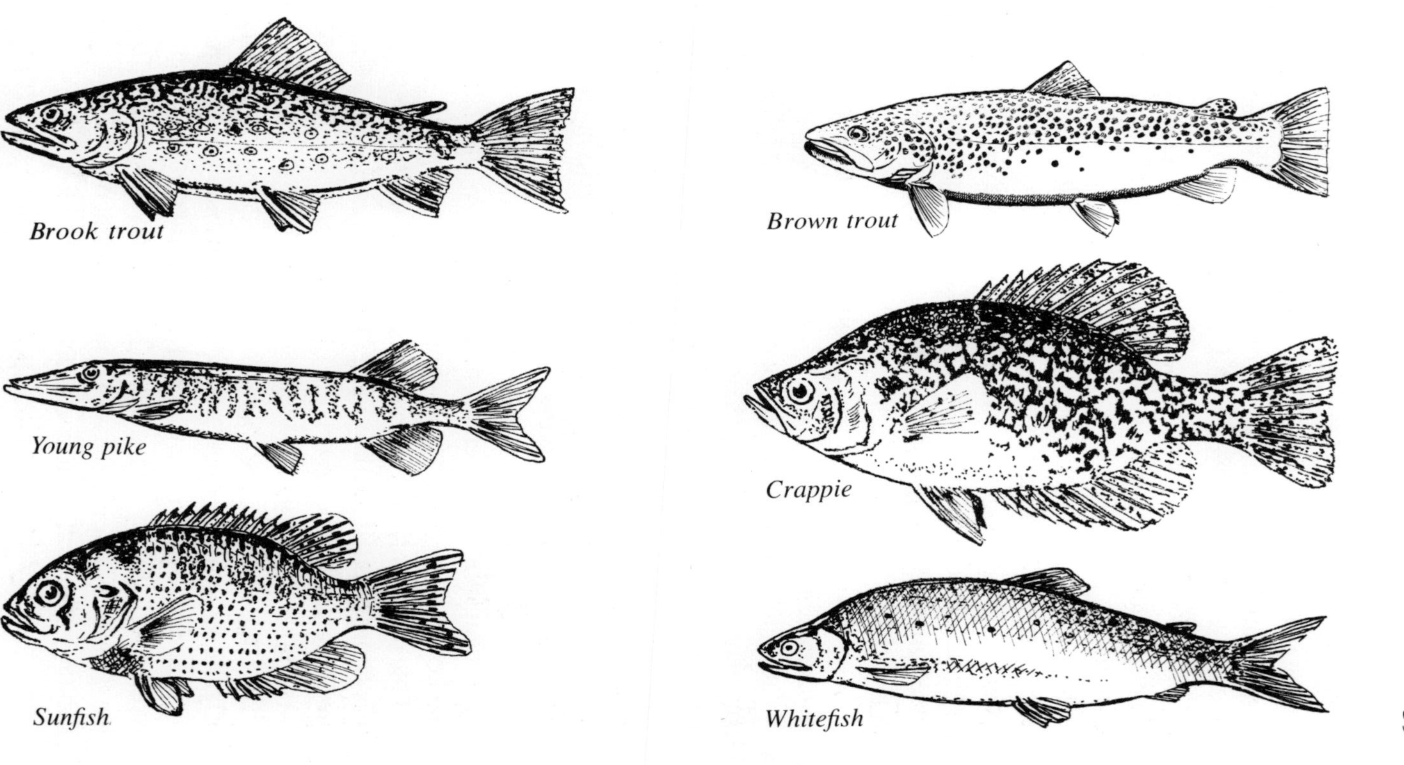
Brook trout
Young pike
Sunfish
Brown trout
Crappie
Whitefish

Pike have been used successfully to control rough fish populations of many different types. Since northerns do not want to work any harder than they absolutely need to in finding food, they quickly begin feeding on the species of fish which is most abundant and specialize on them. It could be bluegills and crappie in a metro area lake or the smelt in the Missouri River system.

The problem many creatures in nature face today is lack of nesting and spawning sites. Given enough space to properly spawn, the pike populations would flourish, however, the swamps and marshes commonly used by pike for spawning tend to lower property values, thus developers and home owners fill in the natural spawning sights. The end result over the course of several years is a decline in pike and a sharp incline in undesirable fish.

Currently much is being done by the Fish and Game Departments of Minnesota, Wisconsin, the Dakotas, Michigan and Canada to restore natural spawning sights that have been destroyed. This program is similar to the Ducks Unlimited projects. Also, targeted marshes and shallow isolated ponds are now commonly used to rear pike from eggs to the fry stage with extremely good success. The use of these isolated ponds make it very cost effective to strip females of their eggs and raise them in a natural environment until they are ready to be stocked in lakes needing a higher population of pike.

One unfortunate occurrence took place as the Missouri River was being flooded to form Lake Oahe and Lake Sakakawea in the Dakotas. As the reservoirs filled, heavy prairie vegetation was flooded forming an ideal spawning habitat for northern pike. Those few years following the formation of the lakes offered some of the finest northern pike fishing for fish fifteen pounds and over the world had probably ever seen, but the writing was already on the wall. Once the lake levels stabilized, the habitat was washed away and the northern pike had poor habitat for natural reproduction. After that, the reservoirs became more suitable for walleye reproduction than northern pike.

Angling success dropped and so did interest in catching northern pike.

Lakes the size of Oahe and Sakakawea are too large in many cases to make stocking a probable means of providing a sportfish, so management methods tend to be designed for the walleye or salmonoid species that would now be better suited for the older reservoirs.

As a whole, fisheries management for northern pike is on the upswing. Things look very bright for the northern pike in regions where they were naturally found and also in other man made lakes where the northern pike is being introduced.

CHAPTER THREE

Seasonal Pike Locations in Lakes and Rivers

As the seasons of the year pass, the relationship the northern pike have with their environment changes to a great degree in some cases. The angler will need to sort through the confusing options which may control the location of big pike.

Part of the problem anglers confront in accepting the watery environment of fish leaves a lot of room for error. The old expression of "thinking like a fish" has some meaning. Spending time out on the water and experiencing northern pike movements first hand can give you the extra edge in finding pike more consistently. In many respects, only time on the water will help you develop what I call "a sixth sense for finding fish." Many times while guiding groups, people would ask why I had selected one spot over another or why this spot was better than the one before. In some cases there was absolutely no reason at all for selecting one area over another, only a "gut feeling." This "gut feeling" is that sixth sense in fishing that only time on the water will teach you.

Many people in the fishing industry claim to have all the answers. It is hard to say if this attitude is meant to help them feel impressive among their peers, or maybe they feel guilty if they don't always have an answer when they are considered the "expert" on the subject. The almost simple logic that can be applied to fishing can work wonders at increasing your success as an angler right from the word go.

Most of the reasons why northern pike move from one place to another, and where they prefer to spend their time has been researched very little. The research that has been done is limited to special lakes or situations. In this respect, personal experience must become a big factor in helping the "would be" pike anglers shorten the time spent between strikes.

In many ways, my task is one that must be thought out carefully and consistent examples, not unique or once in a lifetime experiences should be revealed. Research for this book was conducted all across the North American continent. First hand experience is the only way to put things into proper perspective.

Winter Pike Locations

Much of the primary range of the northern pike exists where ice will be covering lakes and rivers for much of the winter months. The cold water seasons of the year are a growing time for the big females. As soon as the ice melts, they must be ready to spawn.

Ice fishing methods will be discussed later in the book. The winter season is one of the most popular times to get into some big pike action. Some fish, like the largemouth bass feed very little during the winter months, but not the northern pike.

Many of the tricks for northern pike location will depend on the make-up of the lake or river. The one guideline which will help is first knowing where the weedline is or was on the lake. Some lakes have weeds growing to twenty feet, while others have almost no weeds at all. Winter pike tend to feed along or fifteen yards either side of the weed edges. On lakes with no known weeds along the bottom, pike will relate to the steepest or the first major ledge where the bottom contours drop to deep water. In such cases the steepest drop-off you can find to shore will be a well used location by pike.

Pike movement during the winter is far more extensive than walleye or bass. This will explain why short periods of action take place as a group of pike move through. The ideal places for anglers to fish through the ice would be areas that many pike tend to use as a cross-roads for their travels. Radio tracking of pike do show that certain areas are preferred by northerns and selecting these spots with the right equipment is not difficult.

You should first get a contour lake map to give a better basic understanding of what lies below the layer of ice. Your goal is to find an area on the map containing a combination of as many of the preferred factors as possible.

1. Does a creek or river flow INTO the lake? Take special note of this portion of the lake.
2. Is a major point of land protruding near deep water? Select three of the best looking points for this example.
3. Does an inside bend of the lake's contour take place anywhere near the major points or by the river or creek inlet? (Inside bends simply are areas of deep water that extend close to shore)
4. If islands, sunken or above water exist in your lake, is there a portion of shallow water that runs to the nearest shore? (mark these areas).
5. Take note of where any old creek or river beds may be dried up or replaced by drainage ditches or storm sewers that enter the lake.
6. Observe where other anglers are fishing.

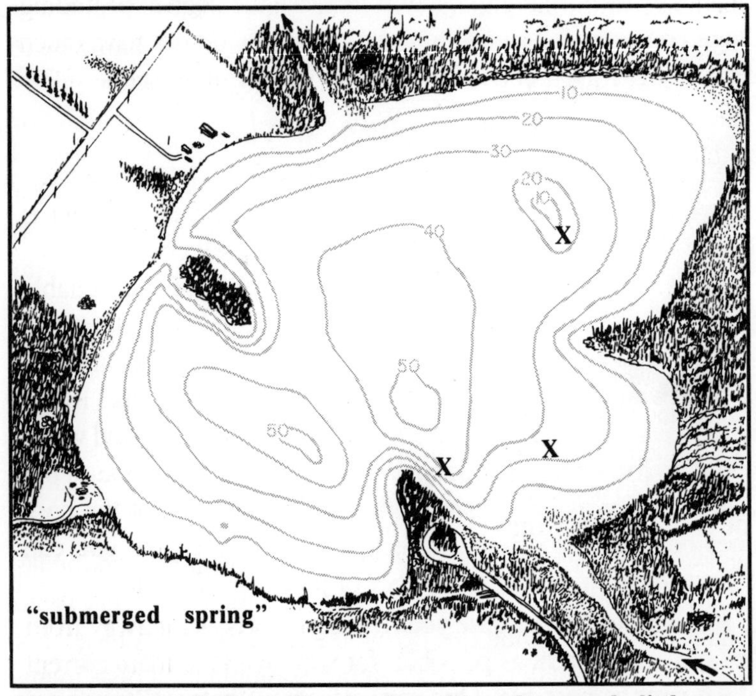

Note locations of winter pike. Anglers will need to spend a little more time locating pike through the ice, but as long as the angler keeps changing depths and areas, pike will soon be found.

Each of the six points listed above can be the sign of a true hot spot. If you find that one area on the lake tends to have two or more of the preferred areas within a short distance, then you have found a good place to begin fishing.

The flasher type depth sounders work very well right through the ice and can be a great time and effort saver. You will want to begin fishing the weed edge or the edge of the first major drop-off. When looking for pike action, run your lines from shallow to deep. When fish are found, run your baits along the same depth levels as your most successful line.

Actually taking the time to fish an area that has potential during the winter months is the only way to properly eliminate water to find fish. When the lake is covered by a layer of ice, you must rely heavily on a good contour map to aid in finding a location which has as many of the locational tips in as small of an area as possible. This will increase the chance of finding large concentrations of fish when you really do not have much mobility to travel all over the lake trying different spots.

River Pike Locations in Winter

River pike during the winter months will seek out the deepest, and largest areas of dead water they can find. Current is one thing winter pike prefer to stay out of at all costs.

Deep, dead water pools off the main channel will enable pike to live in an environment very similar to a lake. Other fish like the bass and walleye also use the same basic areas in rivers to live. It would not be uncommon to find the same pike living in the same pool for the entire winter. These areas of dead water could be five or ten feet deep and range in size from one as big as a house or as large as a football field. The size of the pool does not seem to directly effect the size of the pike you can expect to catch, only the number of pike it could hold.

It is wise to concentrate your fishing efforts as far away from fast moving current as possible. far way from the main current of the river as possible. One very effective "hotspot" on rivers would be the areas very close to the bank. It is possible to find the river is deeper along shore than in mid-stream.

Anglers are warned to use extreme caution when venturing out on any ice, especially frozen rivers.

Winter pike locations in rivers where current is obvious will seek out the deepest areas of little or no current at all.

Spring Pike Locations

The spawning instinct is by far one of the most driving forces a fish has. This is a very important time of year to them and they seem to know it too. Spawning sights are, of course, the key areas to be finding pike, but many states have legislation that restricts angling during the spawning season.Heavy con-

This dandy spring time pike was scarred on both sides of her body.Marks like this are common on both male and female pike in early spring as a result of their spawning activity. Spawning puts a great deal of strain on the inside and outside of a pike's body. In most cases, the pike heal completely within 60 days and look as good as new.

centrations of big female pike can make for some fantastic fishing, as long as the law permits and the fish are released to continue their spawning cycle.

Female pike are, of course, the ones we are after and as winter's cover of ice leaves the shores, the male northern are already heading up to the marshy end of the lake. The first warm rays of spring are used by the pike to sun themselves in shallow protected bays. This is done to help the eggs ripen a little faster. A movement into the shallows goes on in March or early April throughout much of the United States. In regions of northern Canada the pike will be spawning as late as mid-May.

Pike will hold off their spawning areas for no longer than a week. At that time, the pike which are ripe begin to push up the rivers and sloughs to spawn. It is interesting to note that the biggest pike are always the last to spawn. Anglers fishing at this time of year will notice that the biggest fish of the spring are taken right near the end of the spawn.

Once the eggs have been laid the pike like to relax. The female pike could loose 18 to 20 percent of her body weight during spawning and this stress will create a need for rest. Anglers should spend their time in areas just outside the spawning grounds for best success. At this time of year, many of the lakes do not have a thermocline. This means the water does not change temperature the deeper you go. The pike is comfortable at nearly any depth. To the angler, the result could be pike positioning themselves in very deep water.

Female pike will commonly take up position outside the spawning area in waters of 20 to 45 feet. The big pike hold here for a week or two while their bodies recover from the trauma of spawning. They feed very little if at all, but once they are ready to leave the comfort and security of deep water anglers can find some fantastic fishing.

The first move of the deep water pike is right to the same areas the walleye fishermen were in on the opener. It is common for big pike to move into depths even shallower than wall-

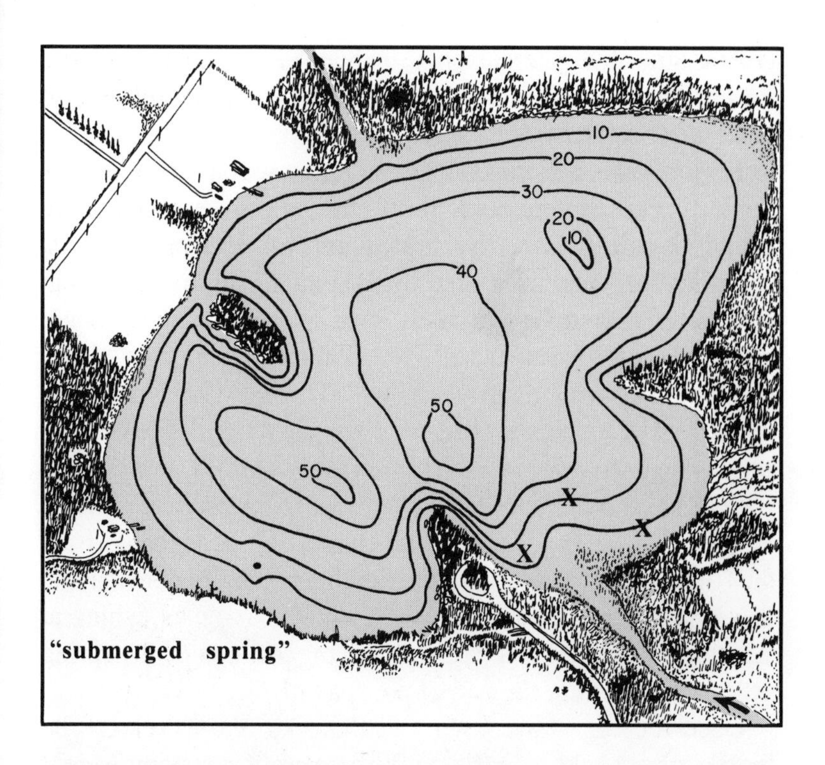

Areas near spawning grounds and in flowing rivers are prime areas to locate large spring time pike.

eyes. The pike move very shallow to feed on the spawning suckers which enter rivers, creeks, or shallow rubble shorelines to spawn. Big pike just love to fill their empty stomachs with a big sucker.

It is hard to predict exactly what stage of feeding or resting the pike are in when you can't fish until the season opens in some areas. This is why it pays to keep an open mind and resign yourself to the fact that you may need a few days to key in on where the pike will be. By focusing your efforts near inlets or marshy bays, the pike will not be far away.

River Pike in the Spring

Springtime locations of river pike find them seeking out the same shallow water weed areas they used for spawning. Rivers do not offer the kind of diversity in habitat as a lake. River pike will be found in unbelievably shallow water that could very well be high and dry come mid summer. Clear water rivers will make the pike seek the deeper pools. They still remain close to any kind of vegetation and not far from their actual spawning grounds. This could account for the lack of prime northern pike fishing in many of our rivers. The fact that river pike spend a great deal of their lives in a small area greatly increases the possibility of cannibalism.

River pike are often overlooked by many anglers, but they often grow very large and are a real challenge to land in a fast current.

Springtime action for river pike is often best in the same area northern may have used for spawning earlier in the year. Some of the best action can come from only a few feet of water.

Summer Pike Location

With the warming of the water after spring, many believe the warmer the water the more the pike feed. This theory makes a certain amount of sense because the metabolism of the pike will be in high gear during the summer and it makes sense that the pike will be then growing the most too. **WRONG!** In looking over countless studies on growth rates over the years, the prime time for the pike to grow is actually before they spawn and again in the fall. Pike location during the summer is open to many theories. It is my belief that since the temperature isn't ideal for the northern's metabolism to function, they sulk during the summer months in the deeper regions of the lake above the thermocline where the temperature is most favorable. Food is very abundant at this time of year, so the pike's comfort is a factor which is important to its location. Although adult pike do indeed grow during the summer, it is about 1/3 their maximum potential for growth compared to other times of the year!

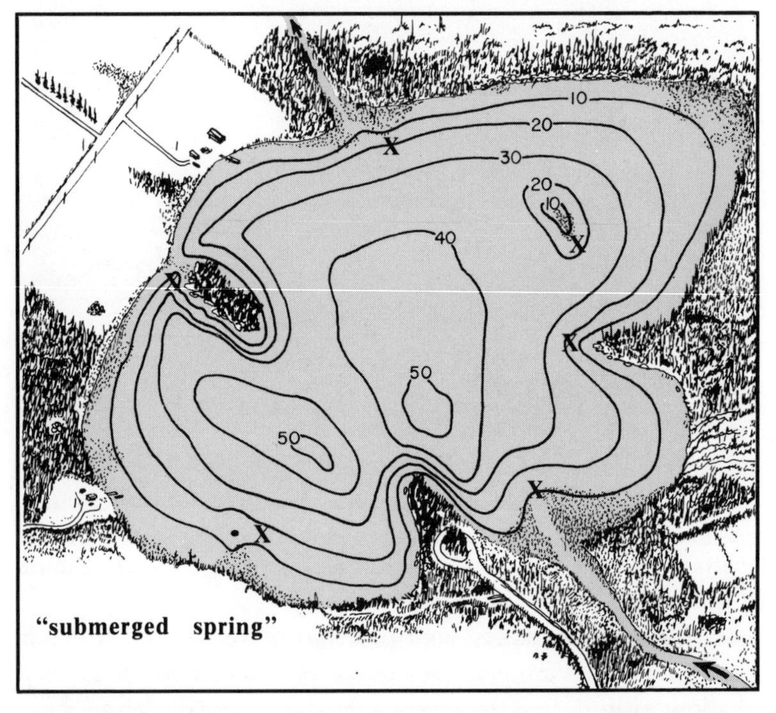

Summertime pike take up positions where they can find food and comfort throughout the day. Isolated areas of unique bottom contours often hold some of the largest pike.

The younger pike under five pounds tend to remain in the shallow protection of the weedline where they are more preoccupied with eating than anything else. This is the group of fish that summertime anglers get into, but the truly big pike that the lake can provide seem to be noticeably absent.

Summer pike definitely relate to the largest points and sunken islands a lake has to offer. Chances of catching a big pike increase if you concentrate around deep water areas that are unique or different. Sunken islands surrounded by deep water, points with deep water nearby, and again the mouth of any creek or inlet that may supply cooler water running into the

In summer, small pike are willing to strike anything that moves no matter what the size. The smaller quick striking pike are almost impossible to avoid while fishing.

lake. On some occasions your lake may be spring fed, in which case the favored temperatures of the pike might be found very shallow even during the extreme heat of summer. Water temperatures coming out of a spring will range from 39 to 44 degrees, which is very different than the summertime water temperatures of 70 to 85 degrees. Finding a spring in a lake is often best done with the aid of special thermometers, but we will be talking more about this later.

River Pike Locations in Summer

River pike in the summer tend to be very current orientated and really prefer to stay out of almost anything that resembles

Current breaks are a key factor for feeding pike. Even the smallest seam of dead water can hold a large pike who may be waiting for a baitfish to be swept into their grasp.

current, but they still realize that the current will bring fresh food and cool temperatures to them as well. Anglers will find grassy undercut banks, where the current seems to break right at the shore or only a few feet out to be the primary holding area for the northern pike. The deep undercut banks on the outside bends of the river tend to be especially appealing to the northern. Anglers will find that pin-point lure accuracy will be a great asset in your success because the pike will not want to venture far in swift current to grab your baits.

Fall Pike Locations

Labor Day is often the beginning of the best BIG northern fishing of the season. The biologists say this sudden feeding frenzy of the big females has been well recorded in studies. The amount of sunlight in a day and not water temperature is the major factor in getting these big pike on a feeding binge.

The best areas tend to be any deep water weed beds or large flat areas of weeds that do not quite reach all the way to the surface. The big female pike are what we are talking about here and at no other time of the year will the chance at taking a wall hanger be as good! Many of the same spots that were fished during the summer and only produced two pounders will be full of ten pounders now. The weed flats do tend to hold bigger numbers of pike, and we have perfected several effective methods for taking these fish as well.

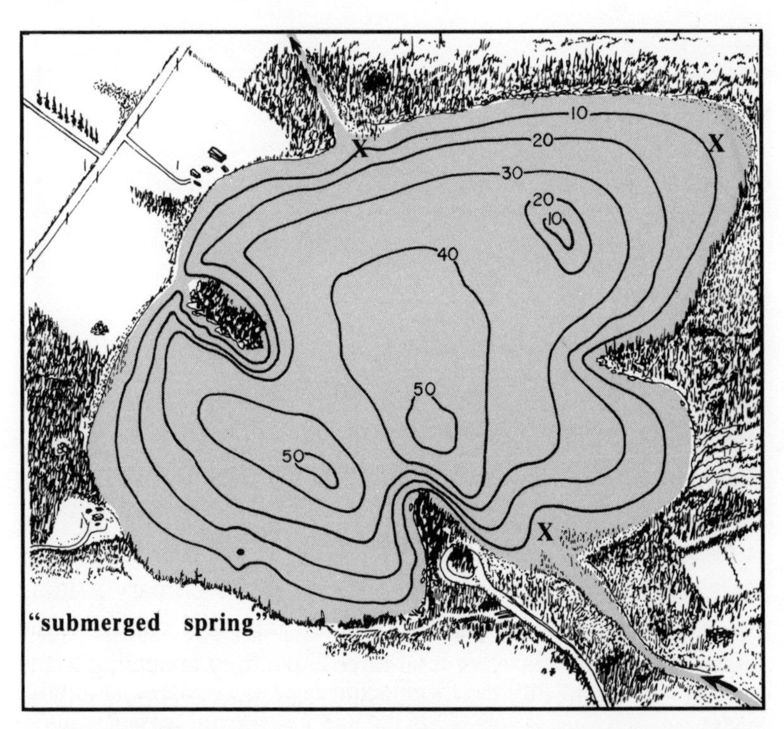

Many of the lakes largest northern pike seem to come alive in the fall. They begin feeding heavily in preparation for the winter.

One of the nice things about fishing at this time of year is the lack of water skiers and other fishermen who lose interest in fishing. Actually, the prime months would be the last two weeks in August and the first two weeks in September. This time is summer by our calendar, but it is the beginning of fall for the big pike. So since it is so distinctly different than the habits of summer fish, we will group it into the fall locational patterns of northern pike.

This major feeding spree of big female pike does not last

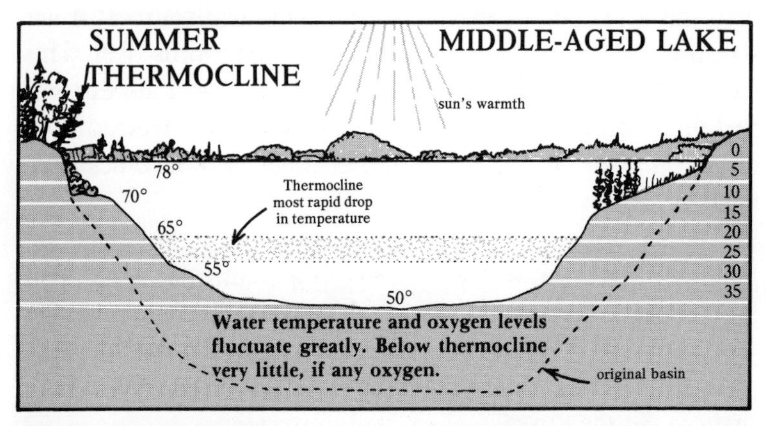

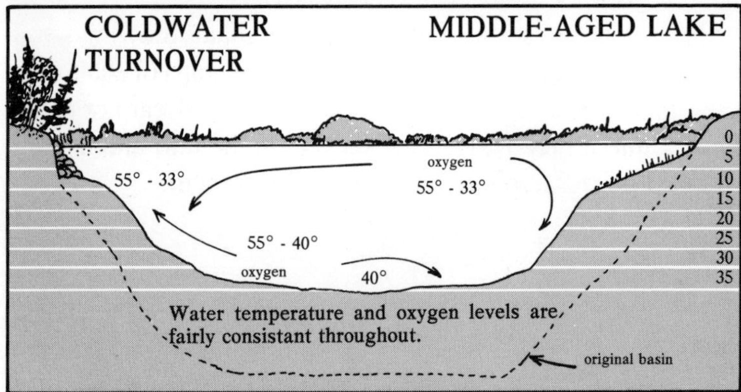

Water temperatures often layer during the summer months when warm water floats above the cold water found deep in the lake. Pike very seldom stray below the thermocline level in a summer lake. The cooler water temperatures of Spring and Fall mix up the water during the "turnover period," which makes it possible for the pike to roam to any depth.

long. Anglers can expect to find this prime condition lasting only a week to ten days at best. After that, your success in summertime locations and large deep water weed flats will drop off dramatically. The signal that the big pike have left the weeds is when they turn brown and begin to settle to the bottom.

Once the pike leave the weedy areas on the lake, they move out to the points and continue feeding. The only thing which slows the fall action down is the "turnover" period. This happens as the surface temperature of the water becomes colder than the water on the bottom of the lake. The warmest water will always try to stay on top, thus the lake turns over. This clouds the water with algae and other dead vegetation that settled to the bottom. The fall turnover will mark a week or two of slow fishing until the lake settles down and becomes clear once more.

Fall has historically been a prime time for big pike and anglers willing to brave the chilling temperatures will get their reward. It has been my experience the worst possible fall weather you can hope for is the most ideal weather for catching big pike. Those beautiful indian summer days of late fall do not seem to get the big pike as excited to strike.

Clean rock or sandy points will be the major drawing areas on a lake to the fall pike and especially those gaps of shallower water that may bridge an island to shore. Any stream or creek flowing into a lake may attract suckers in the fall, and the big pike will go right up into the shallows after them.

Fall Pike in Rivers

In rivers the very same feeding frenzy takes place, but pike will quickly move to the deep water pools they plan to spend their winters in as soon as the first frost hits the air. Again, large dead water eddies are prime spots and remember to fish the areas the farthest from the current.

Fall pike in rivers feed heavily on suckers, which migrate into the rivers during the fall months. Action is good in areas of little or no current.

Conclusion

Northern pike, like all fish will react to changes in their environment, how they react can vary greatly. Every lake or river has its own personality, which in turn affects location and habits of the fish that live in that body of water. Pike do seem to show a desire to frequent the same areas year after year.

Anglers will be pleased to know once a hotspot is found, pike will continue to use it as long as the conditions do not change. Time on the water is the only true way of finding these "honey holes." The shortcuts in location given in this chapter were meant to guide you in the right direction, but you must learn to adapt to the ever-changing conditions at hand and make the best of it.

Weather Effects on Pike

Fishermen can not do too much about the weather. We can hope for calm, cloudy days which are not too hot or cold, but 90 percent of the time the conditions are far from ideal. Anglers looking to make the best of a bad weather situation find the pike the most willing to bite. More than one fishing vacation has been saved by the aggressive attitude of the northern pike when the walleye or bass did not want to bite. The aggressive nature of northerns make them the gamefish least affected by a cold front. Cold fronts follow a major storm system and is best summed up as a rapid temperature drop and very bright skies. A cold front passing through the area can make fishing difficult, but the pike are the least affected of the gamefish by this kind of weather disturbance. A major cold front can easily ruin the summer vacation of a walleye or bass fisherman. This is one of the reasons why the popularity of the northern pike keeps coming on strong. No matter how bad the weather gets, the fishermen can always count on a few northern pike to be ready, willing and able to make your day.

The wind has been found to be a great asset in attracting baitfish for the northern. The ideal situation is a wind of at least ten miles an hour blowing from the same direction for over twelve hours. This intense pounding of waves along the shoreline for prolonged periods will definitely mean the pike can be taking advantage of the higher baitfish concentrations found there. Do not expect the pike to suddenly go crazy if the wind just started to blow into a shoreline. It may not be easy, but fishing on the wind blown shores of the lake can make a difference in catching some nice pike.

Rain seems to get the big pike excited. Many outstanding catches of big pike have been during a driving rain storm. Being out in a thunderstorm is not a wise idea. On those all day rains where the sky is solid gray, the pike are very active.

Anglers should find that they have little need to adjust their locations with a sudden change in the weather. Northern pike are surprisingly consistent in staying around preferred areas, but it may take some adjustment in technique to continue catching fish.

Lake Types

There are many different classifications a lake may fit into from a scientific standpoint. For the fishermen, we can break it into three major groupings. These groupings are very general, but in many cases give at least some idea of how lakes differ in make-up. The key here is knowing that all lakes grow old. It may take thousands of years for a rocky Canadian lake to turn into a swamp, but with enough time, it will.

Young Lakes: These are often referred to as Canadian shield lakes. They are very rocky, clear and the water is very infertile. This means it cannot support a large population of fish. Cannibalism among northern pike is very common in these lakes where it is truly survival of the fittest. Known for being trophy pike waters, these lakes can be quickly ruined by intense fishing pressure. The northern pike live the longest in young lakes, but the total amount of pike is often very low.

Middle-Aged Lakes: This type of lake is often ideal for pure numbers of pike and lakes in this category are traditionally some of the best walleye fishing waters too.
Mostly sand and rubble, these lakes can raise many large pike, but they top out at about twenty pounds. These lakes are often found to have a good population of large and small pike and can make for some good all-around fishing.

Old Lakes: These lakes are very fertile and abundant with many forms of fish. Pike found in these lakes often grow very rapidly for the first half dozen years, but due to the lack of a "high protein" food source like whitefish or ciscoes, the pike

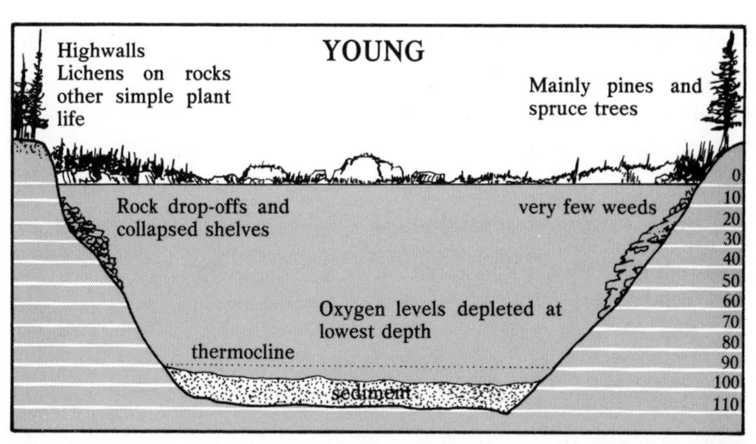

YOUNG
Highwalls
Lichens on rocks
other simple plant
life
Mainly pines and
spruce trees
Rock drop-offs and
collapsed shelves
very few weeds
Oxygen levels depleted at
lowest depth
thermocline
sediment
0
10
20
30
40
50
60
70
80
90
100
110

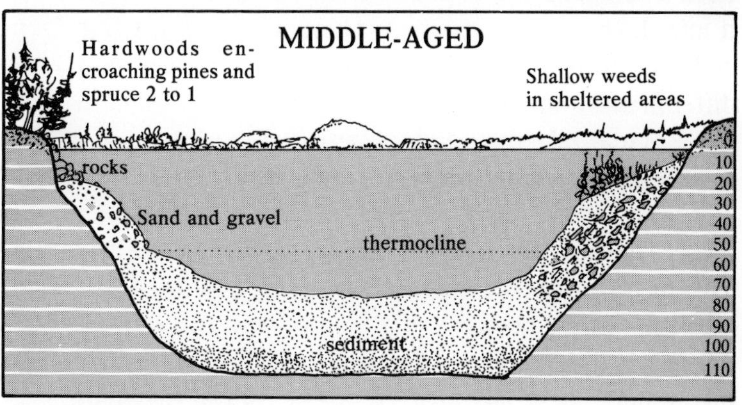

MIDDLE-AGED
Hardwoods en-
croaching pines and
spruce 2 to 1
Shallow weeds
in sheltered areas
rocks
Sand and gravel
thermocline
sediment
0
10
20
30
40
50
60
70
80
90
100
110

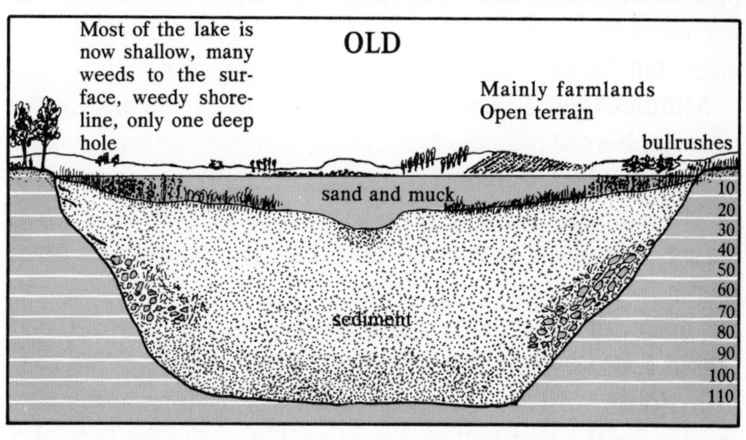

OLD
Most of the lake is
now shallow, many
weeds to the sur-
face, weedy shore-
line, only one deep
hole
Mainly farmlands
Open terrain
bullrushes
sand and muck
sediment
10
20
30
40
50
60
70
80
90
100
110

seem to top out at fifteen pounds. These lakes often are victims of freeze-outs during the winter months because the shallow weed infested lakes can easily become void of oxygen during a long and snowy winter, when the dead weeds decay and absorb the oxygen. Often heavily stocked, these lakes are great for pike five to ten pounds in size. When natural reproduction is present, the pike can quickly become over abundant in a small lake.

CHAPTER FOUR

Tackle Needs for Pike Fishing

Before an angler can hope to catch big pike with consistent success, it is important to realize just how important the selection of equipment can be. A visit to a local tackle shop can often reveal a wide variety of equipment to choose from. Pike fishing demands a lot of special equipment that may or may not apply to other species. That is why each angler evaluate his or her own needs to make the most practical purchases. Fishing can be expensive or as cheap as you wish.

The money you have to spend on fishing equipment does not have to limit the chances of catching pike. In fact, one method of pike fishing we will be talking about later in the book deals with the use of a plain old fashion cane pole! In fishing today, it is very hard to ignore the many different advancements in space age materials and products to make fishing more enjoyable for everyone. To some anglers, there always seems to be another fishing related toy on the market for them to spend their money on, but what will these toys really do to increase your success as a pike angler? In many cases, gadgets and surefire tricks are a little more "show than go," when it comes to actually producing more northerns.

The modern day pike angler has a much wider variety of tackle to choose from than their parents did. This wider selection of tackle has confused many would-be anglers with how to select the proper kind of equipment. At the same time it has opened many new avenues of sportfishing never before enjoyed by our forefathers. In many ways the innovative minds of fishermen have given birth to many outstanding advancements in fishing equipment to make fishing much easier for everyone.

Northern Pike Rods and Reels

The fishing rod and reel for the pike angler today has come a long way in only the last ten years. The introduction of space age rod materials and great advancements in rod design have literally set a new stage in which fishing can be enjoyed.

Looking back thirty years, it would be hard not to specialize yourself with only a few fishing methods as only a few types of rods and reels existed. Thirty years ago, would-be fishermen had a very small selection of fishing outfits to choose from, so certain methods of fishing became the "only" way to go in some regions of the country. If we went back even further yet, fishing was only a "purist's" sport where refined equipment and very involved equipment maintenance was required. This, along with the comparable high cost at the time, had a way of keeping the everyday person out of fishing. Women in the sport were extremely rare and children were just left at home. If anything, advancements in fishing have broken down the barriers of sex and age to make fishing into a sport everyone can enjoy.

In fishing rods today, anglers have a wide variety of designs and materials to choose from. These rods can be made out of fiberglass, graphite, boron or a mixture of all three. These rod materials can greatly effect the total design of a rod. The cost for a good pike rod will also be directly reflected in the material used to make it as well as the way the shaft is designed. The proper selection of a rod will end up meeting two basic requirements, cost and design. It is possible to get a rod that is designed for a particular method of fishing without spending a lot of money. The cost of a rod can be greatly influenced by the quality of the line guides, the way they are wrapped onto the blank and the type of handle used. That is why it is very possible a rod of the same action may be 50% higher in price.

A look at what anglers in other countries use for equipment brings out some interesting possibilities and philosophies on fishing styles. In Europe for example, extremely long rods are used for nearly every kind of fishing. Rods any shorter than eight feet are considered to be "short." While in the United States, pike rods rarely exceed six feet. Longer rods do have some advantages as they give the fisherman better casting range.

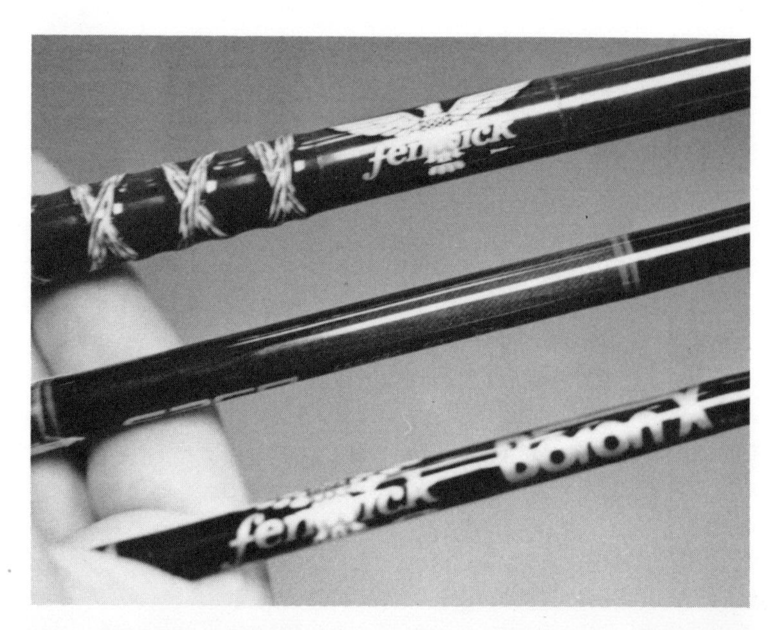

Three different rod shafts all made from different materials. The top shaft is made from fiberglass, the second is made of graphite and the bottom shaft is made of boron. Although the actual size of the rod shaft is very noticeable in fiberglass when compared to graphite, the difference is only slight in performance and size from graphite to boron.

In some cases, better hooksetting power will result with more leverage being put on the fish. Short rods are more manageable to fish artificial lures day in and day out.

They are noticeably lighter in weight and give good casting accuracy at short ranges. These stout rods do a fine job of throwing heavy lures without adding undue stress to the rod or the angler.

One of the major reasons Europeans like to use long rods for pike fishing is the simple fact that pike anglers in this part of the world use live and dead bait fishing methods more than anglers in the United States. A long rod does a superb job of throwing fragile baits and is challenging to play out a large pike as well. Unfortunately, many anglers find one rod which ends up being their favorite and is used for every fishing situation. Whenever equipment not properly balanced with the lures or fishing methods used, it runs a high risk of being damaged. One can only compare this strategy of equipment selection to that of attempting to play golf with only one club! With some fishing methods, anglers will find they demand certain rod requirements, otherwise you will run the risk of damaging or breaking the rod. Where do you draw the line as to when a rod should or should not be used?

Pike anglers should first take the time to evaluate their individual needs and use this as a guideline to follow. First time anglers will be better off reading the chapters on fishing techniques and decide which ones sound the most intriguing or appealing to them. Good tackle shops will have a qualified expert on hand to help make the proper selection of a balanced rod, reel and line combination for your budget.

Before any rod has been selected, we must first decide which type of fishing reel will best fit your needs. There are three basic types of reels on the market today, Spinning reels, spincast reels and level wind reels.

Spinning reels are designed best for light lines, light lures and are ideal in areas where long casts are required. Not a primary choice for the pike angler since spinning reels do not function well with heavy line. Casting and retrieving heavy artificial lures with spinning tackle is difficult.

Spincast reels are very popular among first time anglers because they are easy to operate. Spincast reels lack the ability to handle heavy lines as well. The much slower retrieve ratio common on these reels makes for a poor choice if you plan on doing much casting.

The level wind, or "baitcasting" are commonly used for casting and trolling. These reels are designed to handle heavy lines and cast heavy lures. Although they have had a reputation for being the most difficult reel to use because of their over spin problem, reel makers today have refined the old style baitcasting reels to almost eliminate many of the old problems. First time anglers can now master the use of this reel with only a few minutes practice.

Here are the four major categories of reels to choose from; (left to right) Spincast reels, push button casting makes this reel very easy to master. Spinning reels or open face reels, designed to cast light line and light lures. Baitcasting or level wind reels, often the best all-around choice for pike fishing because it is capable of handling heavy lines for casting. Trolling reels, inexpensive and designed to simply hold line and crank in a fish, ideal for trolling.

To break down the requirements you will need out of a rod after a reel choice has been made is no magical trick. In most cases, the manufacturer has taken the time to tell you what the rod is best designed to do. By looking on the shaft of the rod, just above the handle, you will notice a label that recommends preferred line size and lure weights. By matching your lure weights to a particular rod, you are then free to select one that is a comfortable length for you, and one that falls within your price range.

With many of the preferred pike rods designed to handle lure weights to two ounces, purchasing a rod made of boron or graphite may not be as advantageous as it might be when selecting an ultra light spinning or fly rod. The powerful heavy action rods end up being very close to the same total weight for fiberglass as for graphite or boron. From a fishing standpoint, each manufacturer has a different shaft thickness and taper which greatly effects cost and in the long run, the durability of the finished blank.

A common mistake in selecting a rod type is to mis-match the rod action with the type of lure being fished. A rod which can handle lure weights up to two ounces is a very powerful stick. By mismatching a rod's action with too heavy of a lure, there is a very high risk of snapping the rod in half just by casting the lure alone! On the other hand, if you use too light of a lure, the rod is just no fun to fish and hard to cast accurately.

Many "sportsmen" prefer fishing for big pike with light action rods, it does take practice to properly control a light action outfit as a pike tries to snap your line. There is no doubt this kind of fishing is very rewarding and challenging, but it must be again stressed it is perfectly acceptable to use light tackle when light lures are being used. Anglers MUST learn the limits of their tackle if they hope to get the maximum performance and life out of an outfit.

One very noticeably exception in the "big lure big rod" theory is the use of the long balsa wood lures, these very effective minnow type baits were made popular world wide with the Rapala. This type of bait, although it looks big, is actually very light in total weight, so anglers can get by with fishing them on very light tackle. The fine wire hooks found on these lures almost require anglers use a light action rod to prevent the hooks from pulling out during the battle. This is one lure where the hook setting power in a rod is done with a simple snap of the wrist. A heavy action rod will simply put too much pressure on the hooks and before long they will either straighten out or pull out of the fish.

It would be hard to list every possible rod or reel option without missing a few. That is why anglers should shop at sporting goods stores that can give you advice as to which rods and reels are available in your market area. Stay with products that have a good customer service policy and don't be afraid to ask if they have had any problems with that brand of rod.

For reels, the abundance of quality manufacturers makes it very difficult to select only one. It has been my personal experience with Ryobi reels and their dependability that sets them apart from all other reel manufacturers I have used. In spinning, spincast or level wind reels, the smoothness of action and drag along with trouble free performance, makes the top line of the Ryobi reels simply superb. I must stress the importance in choosing a reel that is the top of the line. These are the reels designed to take the abuse and constant pounding northern pike fishing often dishes out.

Lines, Leaders and Knots

The final link between you and your first trophy northern pike is a fine piece of line, some wire and a few knots. All of which must be assembled correctly in order to land the pike of a lifetime, because you can count on him testing your equipment to the limit.

The members of the pike family are the only fish in fresh water that have teeth capable of biting through your line. Walleye, trout and panfish anglers are reminded **NOT** to use leaders, but pike anglers are literally required to do so if they have any hopes of landing a fish.

One case in point is among the bass fishermen who have found it very advantageous to fish bass without wire leaders. In lakes where both northern pike and bass are present, the bass angler loses many of their best baits to what they call, those "toothies." The same is true with walleye fishermen who run into a few pike while fishing many of the Canadian lakes.

Many anglers choose to play it safe and use a wire leader at all times, just to make sure they do not loose some of their expensive lures. Some anglers feel it is necessary to use leaders whenever they are on lakes with abundant northern pike populations. In doing so, it also must be pointed out that constructing custom made leaders will greatly lessen the effects of fishing with a leader, but still give the needed protection. Designing your own wire leaders in comparison to buying some pre-made types has several over and beyond the money you will save. In many cases the pre-made leaders use inferior components that easily fall apart when you hook your first fish, or worst yet, fall apart just from casting your lures around. Wire leaders should always be made from the strongest components available and **NEVER** compromised.

Do-it-yourself leader kits are commercially available, but in most cases, the components are not much better than the premade versions you would buy. The better tackle shops will stock the individual components needed to assemble quality leaders. Basically, the consumer will have four types of wire materials to choose from.

Coat wires are used in the making of commercially made leaders and tend to be very thick in diameter for the strength of wire. the advantage of the coated wire is that is helps prevent kinking and makes the longest lasting leaders.

Braided copper or stainless steel wire is used by the do-it-yourself leader makers for live bait rigs and other uses where a very fine, but flexible wire is required for best results. This wire is very difficult to work with in many cases, as it does fray and can be easily kinked if not properly stored.

Solid strand stainless wire is very rigid, but is surprisingly easy to work with in short lengths. These wire leaders are used on lures that will be cast. The stiff wire stays away from the hooks and prevents the lure from tangling on the leader. This leader when kinked should be discarded, but are very easy to make and are least expensive of all the leader types. There are also leaders made of extremely heavy guage wire.

In many cases solid strand leaders are made with the same strength wire that is used in the making of many of the popular pike lures. These stiff wire leaders are very popular with muskie fishermen. Mark Windel is one of the major suppliers of muskie tackle in Minnesota and Wisconsin. He markets a solid strand leader made out of spring steel and guarantees them for one full year!

Heavy monofilament is also used to a very limited extent for pike fishing too. Eighty pound test or more in mono can hold up for the first fish or two, but is very prone to shred and weaken with every fish that is hooked. Popular many years

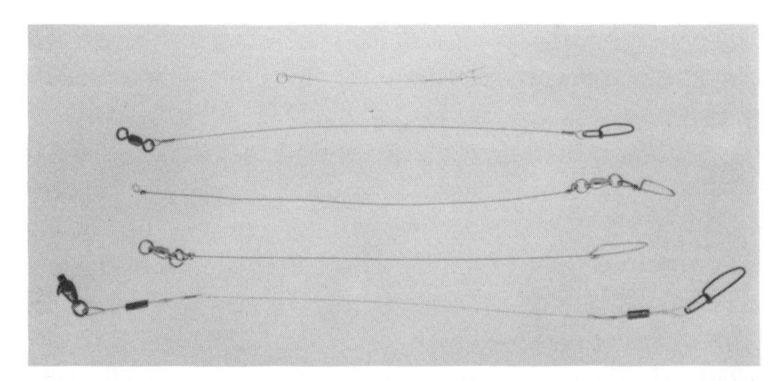

Wire leaders come in many different styles and lengths. Short leaders of under a foot are commonly used for casting, while longer leaders of up to two feet are common for trolling. When large or heavy lures are used, strong leaders are a must, but when small light lures are used, a lighter weight leader makes for a lure with better action.

ago, monofilament leaders are simply not very cost effective when compared to any of the wire leader materials.

Depending on the type of wire used to make leaders, anglers have several different ways in which to attach swivels and snaps. The coated wires for example can be simply melted together for a very secure hold. The braided copper and stainless steel wires demand a brass sleeve which must be crimped onto the line to be secured. The solid strand of wire used in leaders can be twisted to lock in your snap or swivel. (see photo)

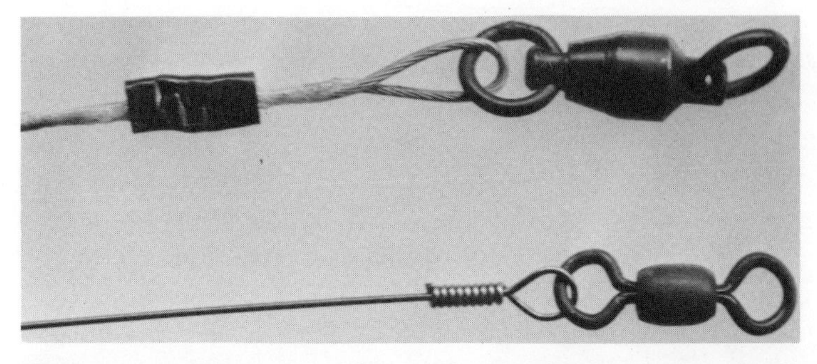

These two leaders were made using two different techniques of securing the ends. The top leader is a coated wire that requires a crimped tubular sleeve. As an added measure, a match was used to slightly melt the coating on the wire to insure a non-slipping loop. With solid strand leaders, all that is needed will be several twists to secure the loop.

The ever popular spoon for pike fishing is the only lure that spins as it is pulled through the water. To eliminate any tangles, a high quality ball bearing leader should be used.

Nearly every commercially-made leader comes with what is called a barrel swivel. These swivels are inexpensive and do a very poor job of stopping line twist. If possible, try to stay away from using this type because barrel swivels also run a very high risk of pulling apart when a pike struggles to get free.

Many fishermen have swivels on their homemade leaders just to make them look more like the commercially tied leaders, but actually swivels are not all that necessary unless you plan on fishing with spoons. A spoon is the one lure where you **MUST** use a ball bearing swivel. With all other lures, swivels are an option. This is why many anglers who make their own leaders prefer to leave off the swivel to eliminate a possible weak link in the leader.

One of the most fragile areas on the leader will be the snap used to connect the lure to your line. On countless occasions, lures and big fish have been lost as a simple snap straightens

***Berkley* Black "Cross-Lok" Snaps. Both ends of snap can be opened. Stainless steel with black flat finish.**

***Rosco* Safety Snap Swivel, Brass Finish**

***Sampo* Muskie and Salmon Swivel. Snap ball bearing swivel, 100 LB test, solid ring and coastlock.**

out or is pulled apart.

In some of my travels to the Northwest Territories of Canada, where anglers expect to hook gigantic pike, one would think fishermen do some planning ahead. Time and time again lures and wall hanging size pike are missed by guys using inexpensive terminal tackle on a trip that would cost a small a fortune.

Remember, your line is only "as strong as it's weakest link," so even though you have thirty pound test line, a cheap snap could very well make your line actually only ten pound test. High quality snaps are hard to find and only one to date is even worth mentioning. It is made by the Berkley Company and is called a Cross-Lok snap. It has a unique double locking system to its bend which helps to insure the snap will not pull out or come unsnapped when the battle is on. Of all the snaps on the market, this is currently the only style of snap anglers can use with a certain amount of confidence. On more than one occasion, anglers have decided to pre-attach the leader to the lure just to avoid the pitfalls of a faulty snap.

***Sampo* Safety Snap Ball Swivel**

Weller
Snap Swivel

***Weller* Ball Bearing**
Snap Swivel

Fishing Lines

The technology of fishing lines has improved over the years just like the rods and reels. The developments of newer and better fishing line materials have made fishing far more trouble free.

It was not all that long ago when anglers were required to hang out their lines to dry after each fishing trip to insure the lines would not begin rotting. Anglers today enjoy the advancements in maintenance free line, but fishing lines of today still have some problems.

Fishing lines on the market fit into three major categories: Braided lines, Monofilaments and wire.

Braided lines have been around the longest of the modern lines. In fact, the braided silk and cotton lines were commonly used by anglers in the 1930's. The only major difference in braided lines of then and now is the material they are made from. Nylon, dacron, and micron are commonly used in the braided lines of today.

Pike anglers fishing casting or trolling heavy artificial lures prefer lines with little or no stretch to them. Line stretch can greatly hinder your ability to get a large treble hook into the boney jaw of a big northern. The braided dacron lines are a real favorite among many such anglers. Braided micron has a smaller diameter for the same comparable line in dacron, but it has a higher stretch factor. Nylon is also used, but it has the largest diameter for its size and has a great deal of stretch. As you might guess, the nylon lines are the least expensive of the three. Nylon lines seem to be a tradition among many anglers and that appears to be the major reason for its popularity.

Monofilament lines tend to have a stretch factor far too great for many of the avid pike anglers, but it has many, positive advantages as well to make monofilament an excellent line material. One not so obvious advantage is found when a lot of casting is done. Braided lines tend to absorb water and as it clings to the line, each cast sprays the angler with water. Although monofilament lines are fragile to nicks and abrasion, they are still more abrasion resistant than any of the braided lines. Anglers wishing to use light tackle will find spinning reels and monofilament lines the best choice. A limited amount of line stretch can often become a safety valve to act as a cushion if a fish makes a sudden run. Successfully hooking a pike with monofilament line depends greatly on just how hard the hook is set and the distance the fish is at when it strikes.

Premium quality line like Dupont's Stren would be an excellent choice in a brand of monofilament. Line color has NO effect on northern pike fishing success, and that goes for the braided lines as well. This is a big topic of debate for walleye, bass and trout fishermen, but there is simply no need to be all shook up about the fish's ability to see your line when we are talking northern pike.

Wire lines are used exclusively for trolling, some are braided wire while others are solid strands. These lines are designed for a more specialized method of pike fishing we will be talking about later. Fishing with wire demands special reels and rods with roller guides to help prevent wire crimping. The use of wire line on pike is getting to be very popular in some areas of the county, but it is still a very specialized style of fishing. Kinking the wire is a problem anglers must be on the watch for at all times.

Line wear is the hidden danger in all fishing lines that can greatly reduce line strength. Actually there is no real way of preventing line wear, it is almost inevitable with every trip you take in search of a record pike. Keeping a watchful eye for weak areas which commonly occur within the first three feet of the line will prevent many of the unfortunate mishaps of line breakage.

Many veteran anglers cut off a few feet of line and re-tie the line to the lure after each fish to prevent loosing a large fish when it does hit. These anglers have learned from experience that "an ounce of prevention is worth a pound of cure!"

Fishing Knots

Learning to tie a good knot for fishing should be learned while at home, so you will not need to waste precious fishing time trying to master a new knot. Anglers should be able to tie their favorite knot in the dark as a good test. Fishermen will of course not need to learn all the various knots in this book, but each does have a special purpose that can come in handy if the occasion arises. (see diagrams)

WORLD'S FAIR KNOT

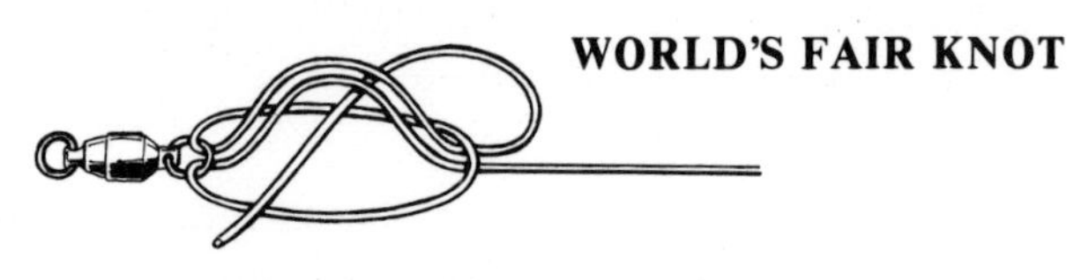

A. Double a 6-inch length of line and pass the loop through the eye.
B. Bring the loop back next to the doubled line and grasp the doubled line through the loop.
C. Put the tag end through the new loop formed by the double line.

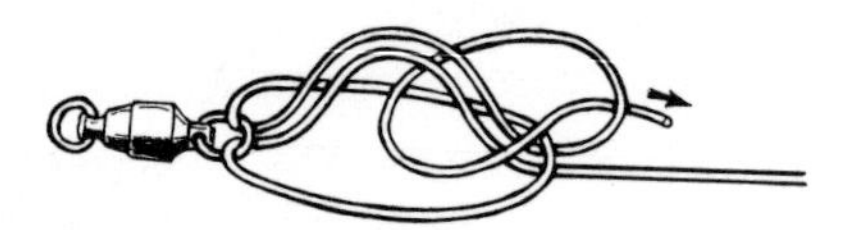

D. Bring the tag end back through the new loop created by step C.
E. Pull the tag end snug and slide knot up tight. Clip tag end.

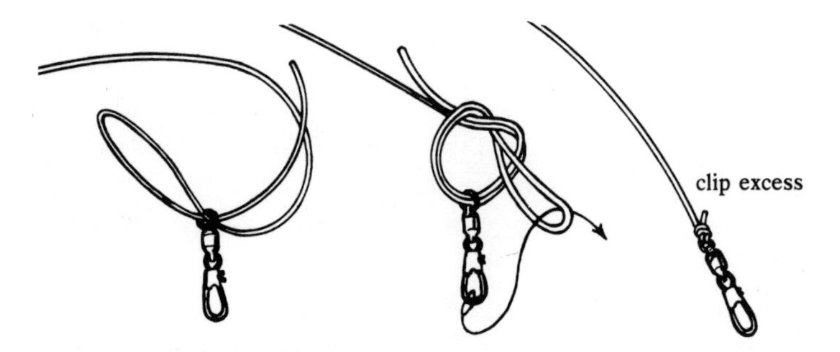

The PALOMAR KNOT is considered to be one of the strongest knots known to tie on terminal tackle. The double wrap of mono insures a strong connection and a strength factor of 85 to 95 percent of the original line strength when tied properly.

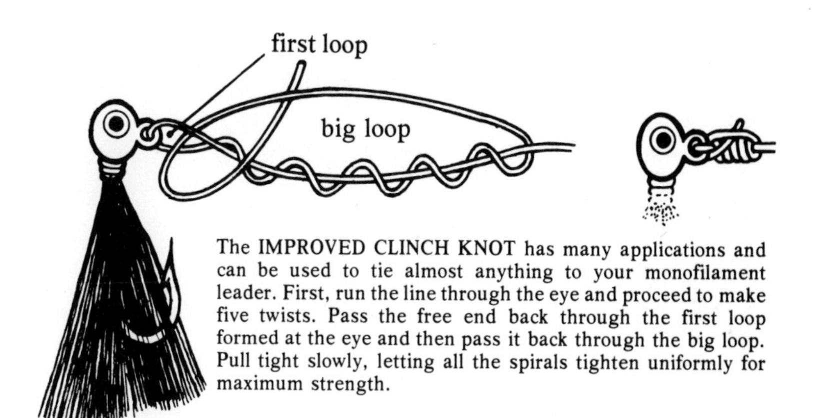

The IMPROVED CLINCH KNOT has many applications and can be used to tie almost anything to your monofilament leader. First, run the line through the eye and proceed to make five twists. Pass the free end back through the first loop formed at the eye and then pass it back through the big loop. Pull tight slowly, letting all the spirals tighten uniformly for maximum strength.

Jansik Special

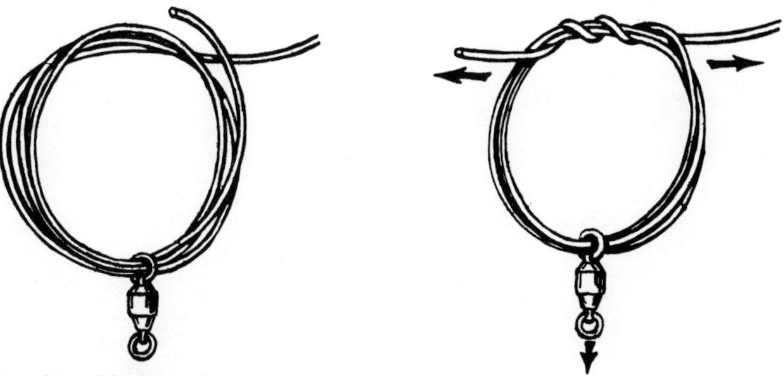

Run about 5 inches of line through eye of hook on lure; bring it around in a circle and run it through again.

Bend standing part of line around the two circles. Bring tag end around in a third circle and wrap it three times around the three parallel lines and draw tight.

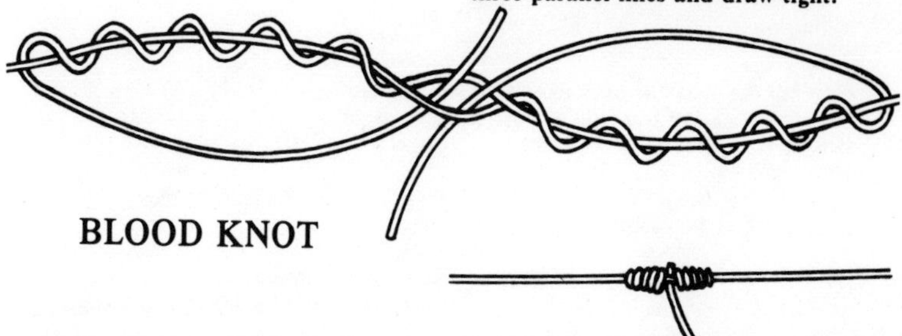

BLOOD KNOT

Want to join two pieces of line together? Use a BLOOD KNOT. When twisting, use five turns on each side, making sure they are in opposite rotations. When the knot is correctly formed as shown, pull it tight and clip off the excess.

Surgeon's Knot

This knot joins a leader to line just like the Blood Knot, though where lines vary in diameters.

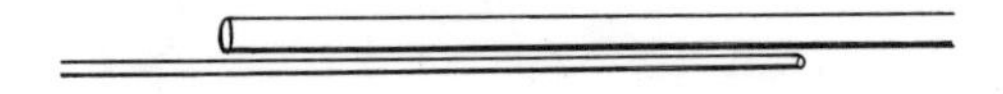

A. Lay line and leader parallel, overlapping 6 to 8 inches.

B. Treating the two like a single line, tie an overhand knot, pulling the entire leader through the loop.

C. Leaving loop of the overhand open, pull both tag end of line and leader through again.

D. Hold both lines and both ends to pull knot tight. Clip ends close to avoid foul-up in rod guides.

Albright Special

This knot is used for tying a light line to a heavy monofilament leader or a wire leader.

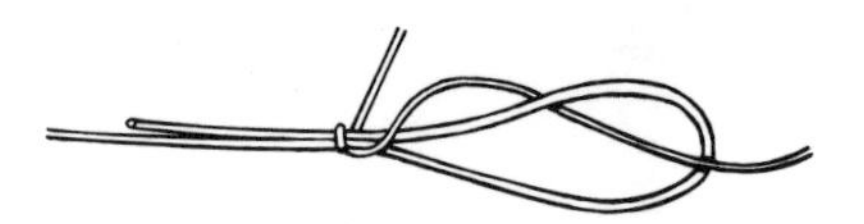

A. Double back a couple inches of the heavy line and insert about 10 inches of the light line through the loop in the heavy line.

B. Wrap the light line back over itself and over both strands of the heavy line. While doing this you are gripping the light line and both leader strands with the thumb and finger of your left hand, and winding with your right.

C. Make ten turns, then insert the end of the line back through the loop once more at the point of original entry.

D. Pull gently on both ends of heavy line sliding knot toward loop. Remove slack by pulling on standing and tag ends of light line. Pull both standing lines as tight as possible and clip off excess from both tag ends.

HOW TO CREATE A NON-SLIP LOOP IN BRAIDED LINES.

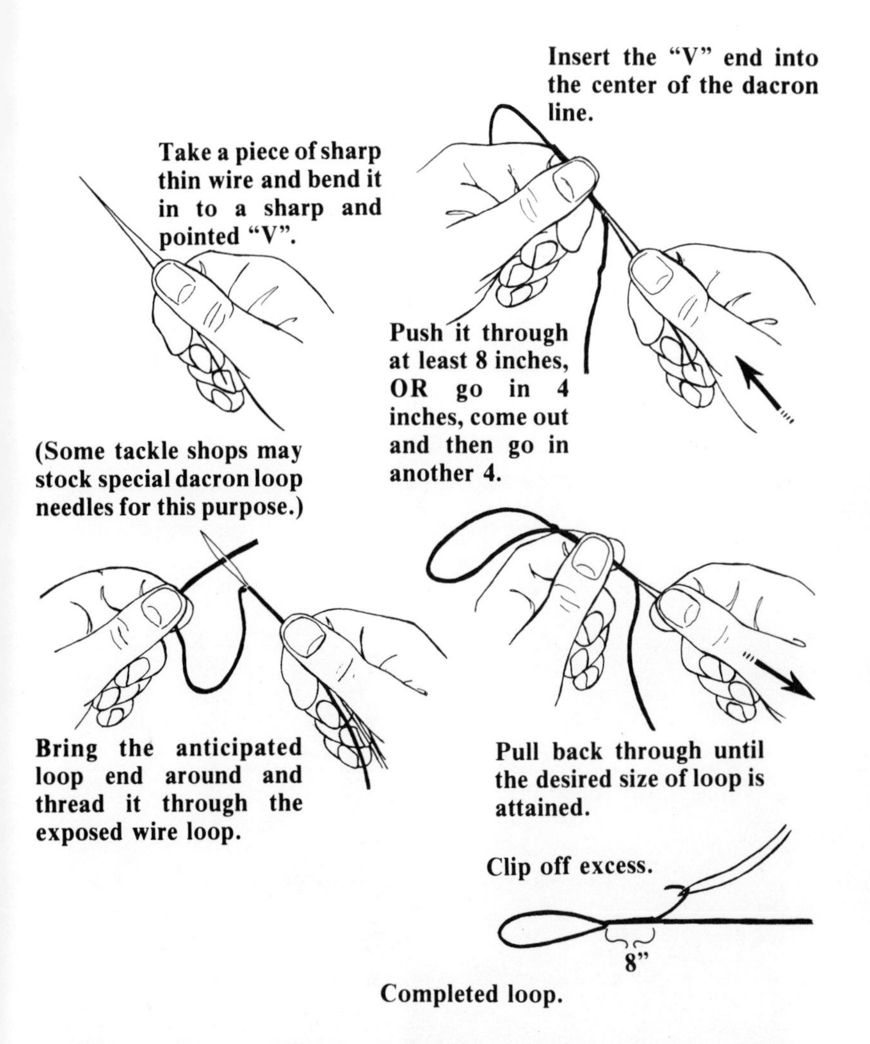

Completed loop.

NOTE: This loop will now replace any need to tie knots in braided lines. To attach the leader or lure, be sure the loop is made large enough to be inserted through the eye or swivel and able to loop around the item you will want to attach.

CHAPTER FIVE

Artificial Lures

This chapter deals with the wide selection of ever changing artificial lures which anglers can choose from to catch pike. We will also be discussing various modifications to current lures to make them more fish appealing.

When we try to appeal to one or more of the northern pike's instincts to feed, we are also trying to match the proper lure with the proper conditions. In almost all situations, there are often many possible lure combinations that will work. Saying one lure is better than another in all situations is being short sighted.

One of the truly great things about northern pike is their willingness to attack a wide variety of artificial lures. One of the major reasons they are so easily taken is that pike rely on

A bit too far! Northern pike have been known to feed on a wide variety of critters, but this giant mouse lure we hope was just a joke.

eyesight to feed more so than other fish. Studies done here in the United States point to the interesting fact that northern pike very seldom feed at all during the night! This could be related to their preference to actually see their prey. In the family of artificial lures, we have basically four types of lures to choose from, spoons, plugs, spinners and jigs. Selecting the correct lure for the current water conditions does not demand a lot of on the water experience, just the knowledge of what kind of action a lure has. Anglers are always advised to keep an open mind when using artificial lures and ready to try any new modification which comes to mind in catching pike in your individual situation. In the family of spoons, there are countless varieties to choose from. One well known tackle shop in central Wisconsin keeps over 75 different kinds of spoons in stock at all times! You have fat spoons, skinny spoons, long spoons and short spoons. All of these spoons have a special purpose where they each can be extremely effective. It is a safe bet to say that any spoon in existence today can catch a northern pike! Thin spoons sink very slowly when pulled through the water and are ideal in areas where you may want to fish above weeds or in

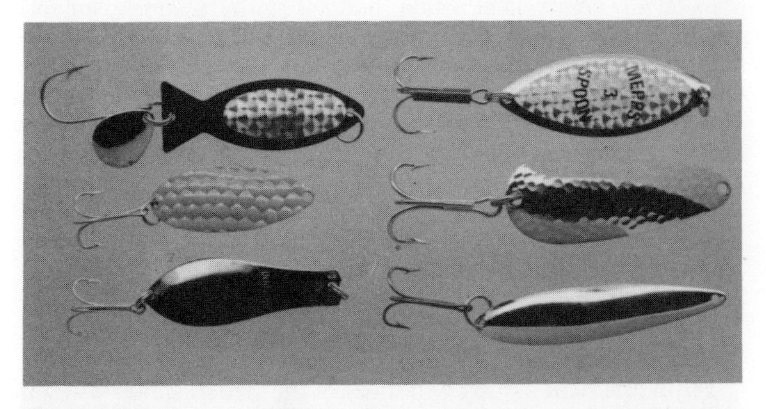

Spoons come in many different shapes and sizes. Selecting a spoon that will best suit your needs may get a little confusing at times. It is important to match the proper spoon weight with the tackle and rod used to throw it to avoid damage. Color and shape of the spoon selected is really not as important as knowing if it will run at the proper depth. The key to catching pike with spoons is selecting a model that will run at the correct depth.

places where a slower lure speed will make it easier for the pike to spot.

Thick spoons can be cast a country mile! If you are looking to improve the distance you can cast from shore or boat, this spoon will perform very well. A thick spoon is ideal in clear water lakes where anglers can use the heavier spoons to run along the deeper weedline edges where pike can often be found.

Spoons, which have a long thin shape are designed to be used for trolling. The fluttering side-to-side action is best achieved when the spoon is being pulled steadily along. These spoons are very thin and light weight, making them impractical to use for casting.

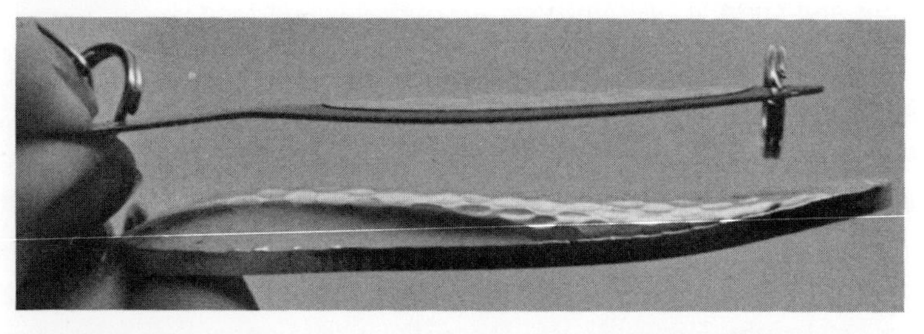

The photo above shows a typical trolling spoon. This paper thin piece of metal has an excellent action, but will run very shallow unless a small weight is added in front of the spoon to keep it deeper. The thick spoon on the bottom is going to sink like a rock when it hits the water. If there is a need to get the spoons down deep, then this would be an excellent choice. Anglers looking to purchase some spoons for pike fishing should be sure to have at least three different weight spoons to run at different depths.

The size of spoon selected for best angling success will range greatly by the type of water you are fishing. For lakes with a heavy pike population in the two to eight pound range, anglers have the best success with spoons two to three inches long.

From practical fishing experience, the size of spoon you will use often reflects the size of pike it will attract. This rule of "big lure, big fish" is rather risky to make a hard and fast rule about as the smaller northern pike will often hit anything that moves, no matter what the size! On the other hand, if only a two inch spoon was used for an entire year, the average size pike you would have caught would be dramatically less than if a spoon of six inches in length were used.

Fishing with a large spoon all the time is rather difficult, because it does demand heavy tackle and the ambition to drag around a large lure all day long. Most anglers find that the smaller spoons of two to three inches in length are the most practical and productive to use on a daily basis.

The colors of a spoon can come in every conceivable pattern. All have had their moments of success, but the traditional red and white spoon is still the most popular color combination ever developed.

Spoons with a hammered or rough finish will reflect more light and sparkle brilliantly as it flutters through the water. Many anglers believe the sparkling will greatly enhance the odds of a pike finding the spoon. No real argument can be made pro or con in regards to this statement. Examples of this theory working and not working can be easily found. What is important is to experiment with color combinations until you are catching pike! Dark days will mean the selection of a darker colored spoon, bright days will often require a very light colored spoon. In waters that are heavily stained, like those found in Canada or in rivers, fluorescent colors tend to be more productive.

Not all spoons are built or designed with the proper color patterns you personally think might work, or have the kind of hooks and "o" rings that will hold up to a day of fishing.

Since many of the spoons on the market are priced more to sell than to catch fish, some steps may be needed to insure that a trophy pike does not get away!

Small, inexpensive "o"rings that connect the hook to the spoon often need to be replaced with heavy duty ones that will not easily pull apart when a pike begins thrashing. The hooks often require sharpening or even replacement after only one fish because the metal in the hooks is soft. Custom lure changes in finish can be easily done with finger nail polish in the colors you like. To add fluorescent colors is is best to coat the new color with clear finger nail polish to protect the finish. Another option commonly used to customize a spoon is a special metallic colored tape available at many tackle shops in a variety of colors. These strips can add extra sparkle to one or both sides of the spoon. Adding an extra wiggle or action to your lure is easily done by adding one of those curly tail rubber worms. The smaller two inch rubber grubs with the curly tails are attached directly to the rear hook by threading it onto one or more of the three treble hooks. This is a trick used by muskie fishermen, but pike anglers will benefit greatly by this tip as well.

Remember!

When trolling or casting a spoon, anglers are reminded they **MUST** use a quality ball bearing leader to avoid line twist.

Northern Pike Plugs

The category of "plugs" for pike fishing is large and covers a wide spectrum of lures for the angler to use. The name "plug" itself is rather outdated by today's standards of razzle-dazzle terms. The new term "crankbait" was invented to help the modern day angler feel something new was in the offering.

"Crankbaits" Here are a few of the baits often used by bass fishermen, but are very effective for pike as well: (left to right) Normark "Fat Rap," Mann's "Deep Pig," Rebel "Deep Wee R," Bagley's "Small Fry," and Bomber "Model A."

The first plugs were made of wood, but today the vast majority are constructed of various plastics. These new space age lure materials are in many cases better and much more durable than wood models, but lack many of the more desirable qualities of flotation and weight. For this reason, many of the more traditional lure companies have continued to make lures made from wood.

The basic concept behind the use of plugs involves three major groups, all of which are designed in some way to imitate a form of baitfish the pike maybe looking to feed on.

The rainbow smelt is a real favorite of the northern pike. Anglers commonly use smelt for dead bait rigs because of their great pike attracting smell.Anglers also do well to imitate this fish with long thin plugs like the Rapala.

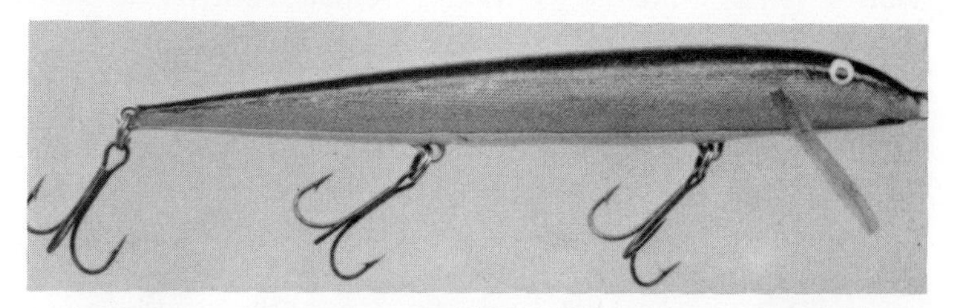

First, there are the topwater lures which act as injured baitfish floundering on the surface. Second, the swimming types that can be either cast or trolled through areas where pike may be feeding. Last, but not least, you have the deep divers which are built mostly for trollers who want to get baits down to the bottom.

How the front of the lure is designed can determine which category the plug will fall into. **(see page 87)** A consumer looking to purchase a few plugs should be aware that topwater and deep diving lures are used very little in most pike fishing situations. Eighty percent of the time the lures in the free swimming category make up the "bread and butter" plugs used by anglers today. Lures like the Rapala, and many of the bass

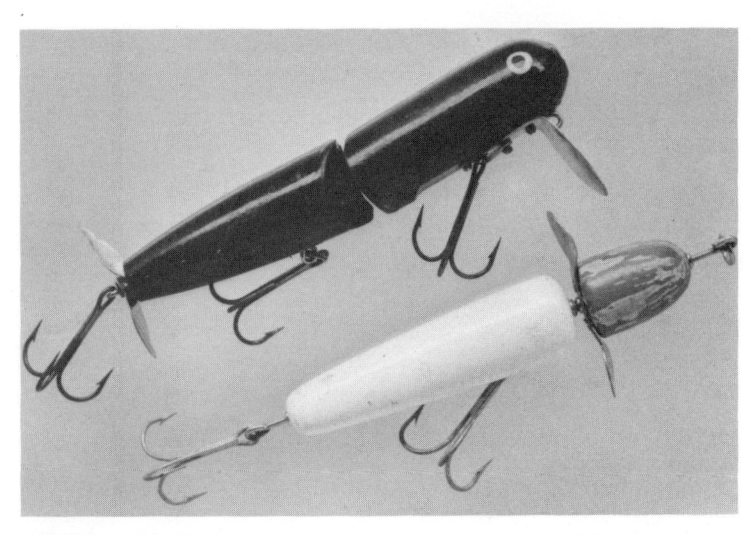

Topwater plugs have limited success on northern pike, but in some areas where pike action is found in shallow water, anglers can have the time of their lives catching pike. The top lure is a Mouldy's Hawg Wobbler, the other is called a "Globe." Both are effective muskie baits as well.

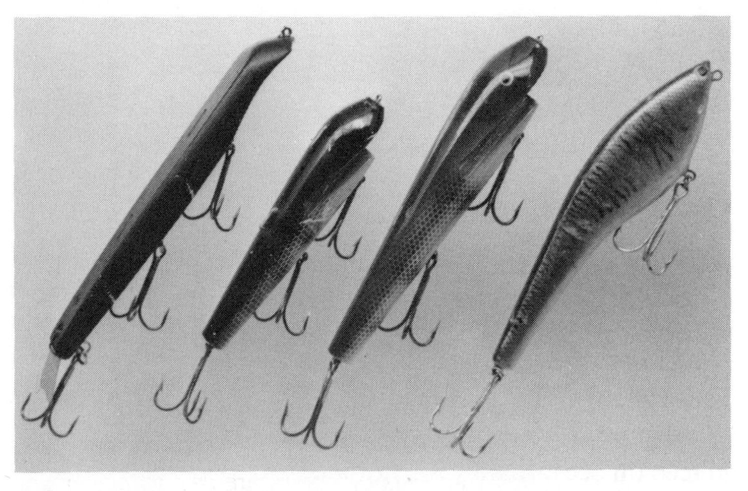

These are called "jerk" baits, but are also known as being an excellent lure for large northern pike. (left to right) Suick, Reef Hawg (small), Reef Hawg (regular), and the Bagley's "B" Flat Shiner. This family of lures are often fished with short jerks to resemble an injured baitfish.

The front lip of a plug determines just how deep it will run. The larger the blade, the more downward resistance they will have as they are pulled through the water. some plugs, like the type shown on the far right side do not even have a lip. The slant of the lures head makes for a tight wiggle action, and will run extremely shallow. Any plug with a metal lip, is designed to travel at faster speeds without running out of tune.

fisherman's popular "crankbaits" fall into this grouping.

The finishes on these types of lures have been developed in recent years more to catch the fisherman than the fish. True to life detail on each and every lure looks great in the package, but do these finishes actually attract more fish? Probably not, but it is much easier to have confidence in a lure which looks more lifelike than the real thing!

As with spoons, the colors to select in plugs will often tend to be very visible. Silver, chrome, and gold make up the most popular colors used today.

Northern pike also show a preference for long and skinny baits instead of short and fat ones. This is probably due to the fact that panfish are the least desirable of the food fish for pike to feed on because they are just too hard to swallow.

How long is long? The ever popular Rapala lure is one of those long and skinny lures that pike really love, and here the best sizes are five to seven inches in length. This size group will be the most productive. If you are after only very big pike, you may find eight to ten inch models slightly more productive. Here again, like with the spoons, it is highly recommended that heavier tackle be used to handle extra large lures.

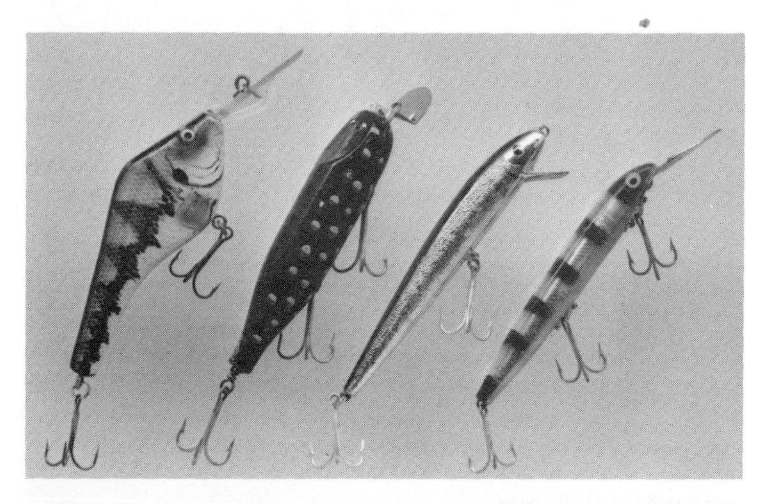

Large Northern pike plugs often resemble different forms of bait fish. Some plugs are so large and hard to pull through the water that trolling is only the practical way to use them.

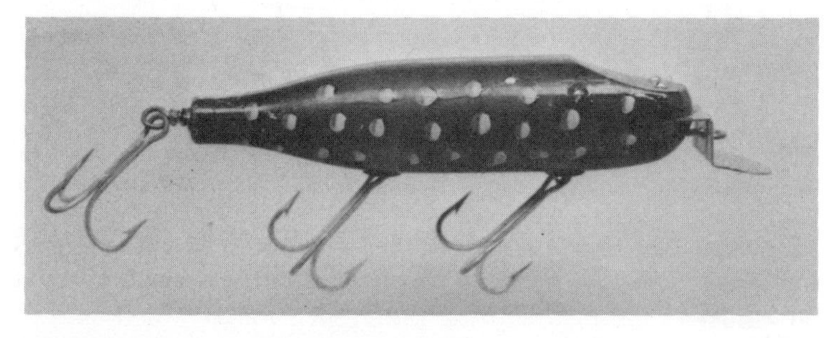

To customize your own plugs, simply re-paint the lures with color combinations you think will be the unfair advantage. This pikie minnow is a real favorite with northern fishermen, but can easily become chipped or chewed up by the sharp teeth of the pike. A coating of epoxy will lock in colors and put a hard finish on the lure that could extend the life the the bait.

Large pike like this one are often taken with bucktails. Many anglers who prefer to cast for northern pike find spinners extremely effective for big pike.

Spinners for Pike

This group of lures is one of the most popular and is considered by many as one of the best ways to catch a big pike. Designed to run no deeper than about three feet, this family of lures includes the ever popular Mepps spinners and many of the newer spinnerbait designs that bass fishermen love so much.

The in-line spinner, like the Mepps, has a bucktail skirt around the hooks to give the lure body and extra action. When combined with a large spinning blade, this lure has all the ingredients of a large creature, from the fishes point of view. That is why many muskie fishermen use these in-line spinners as one of the best fish catchers in their box. Often referred to simply as a "bucktail" these baits are very easy to pull through the water for their size and has become the #1 big fish bait among many anglers because they can cast these baits all day without tiring. As one wise fisherman once said, "you can't catch a fish unless your bait is in the water!"

Bucktails are one of the real favorites among pike anglers. Shown here are some "in-line" spinners that are popular. The Windel's Harasser, Fudally Hawg Tail and Ted's Bucktail.

The spinnerbait style of spinners is more difficult to pull through the water than most in-line spinners. It has the advantage of being almost weed free because the wire arm supporting the spinner acts as a keel to protect the hook as the bait runs over weeds or snags. The single hook concept of the spinnerbait will demand anglers set the hook harder to successfully land a hard fighting pike. Anglers commonly modify these types of spinners by adding an additional hook behind the large main hook. This is referred to as a trailer and can do wonders for catching pike on days when they just seem to have a rough time grabbing your lure properly (see photo).

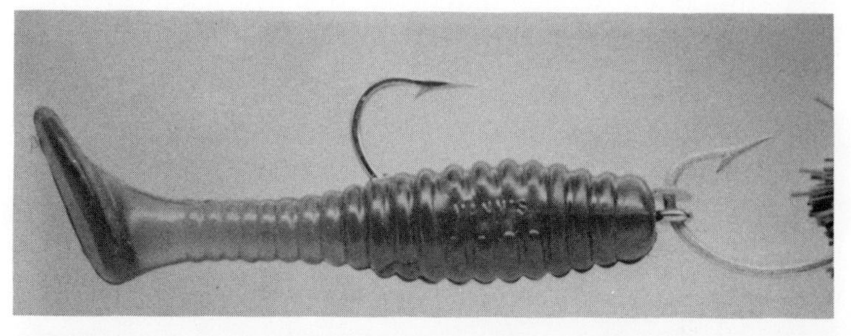

Attaching a trailer hook to the back side of a spinnerbait is recommended whenever possible. This trailer hook needs to have an eye large enough to slip over the barb of the main hook and is prevented from sliding back off the hook by a small piece of plastic or rubber.

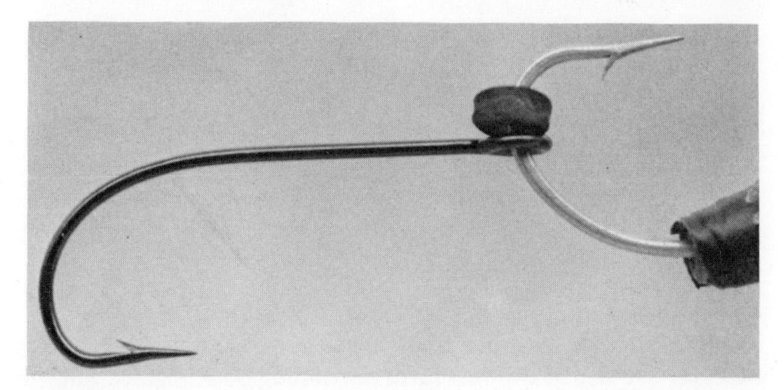

One little tip for anglers fishing for pike in areas clear of weeds, is to attach the trailer hook so that it points downward. This makes it easier for the pike to be hooked in the soft bottom jaw when they come from under or behind the bait to strike.

The size of spinnerbait you select can vary from 1/8 ounce models for smallmouth bass to three ounce models that muskie fishermen use. Pike anglers also have the option of single spinner or tandem (two) spinners on the wire. The single spin models are not used by pike anglers who prefer the maximum amount of flash and vibration out of a bait. The tandem spinners are commonly used in heavily stained lakes and rivers with great success. The larger the spinnerbait, the more it is required that a strong outfit is used to throw it about. One ounce models are considered by many as the small size for pike and muskie. Although these spinners are much more work to throw around, they still do an excellent job of catching fish. You can troll or cast these spinners as well, but many prefer them for casting as spinnerbaits can be cast into thick weeds and other obstructions where some big pike maybe lurking.

The blades on a spinner are often painted or modified in some way to do a better job of catching fish. In stained water where sunlight does not penetrate much more than a few inches,

Giant spinnerbaits made with bucktail or rubber skirts are very effective on northern pike. They come in a variety of styles, some have one single hook while others may have two sets of large treble hooks. The faster a bait is fished, the more critical it will be to have treble hooks on a lure. These baits are also grouped into the "bucktail" family of baits. The spinnerbaits above are all made by the Fudally Tackle Company of Minneapolis.

The "Buzz Bullet" spinnerbait made by the Lund Lure Company is one of the best choices among the bass type spinnerbaits for pike fishing simply because they are built with the highest quality components and can take the abuse a big northern pike may give. Another great feature of the "Buzz Bullets" are their ability to change blade sizes to give the bait a different action and vibration. Bigger blades slow the bait down and help keep it near the surface, while smaller blades permit the lure to travel at faster speeds and sink into deeper water.

a fluorescent color added to the blade permits it to give off a color that is visible even if the sunlight can not reach the blades. White, orange and silver blades make up the majority of colors used by pike anglers.

Bucktail covered treble hooks are commonly found on in-line spinners and only the largest of the spinnerbaits. Black bucktail is by far the most popular color with white, yellow and red far behind in popularity. Many of the spinnerbaits have rubber skirts instead of bucktail hair. It seems fishermen tend to prefer the traditional hair for pike over the new rubber skirts. This trend will likely change as the rubber products continue to improve.

Again, there are little things you can do to a factory made spinner to make them a little better. The addition of curly tail rubber worms is again a good idea **(see page 94).** It is very easy for the razor sharp teeth of the pike to cut through the wrappings that hold the bucktail on your hook. By adding a clear epoxy mixture or just clear finger nail polish, a protective coating can be placed over the wrappings to make them much more durable.

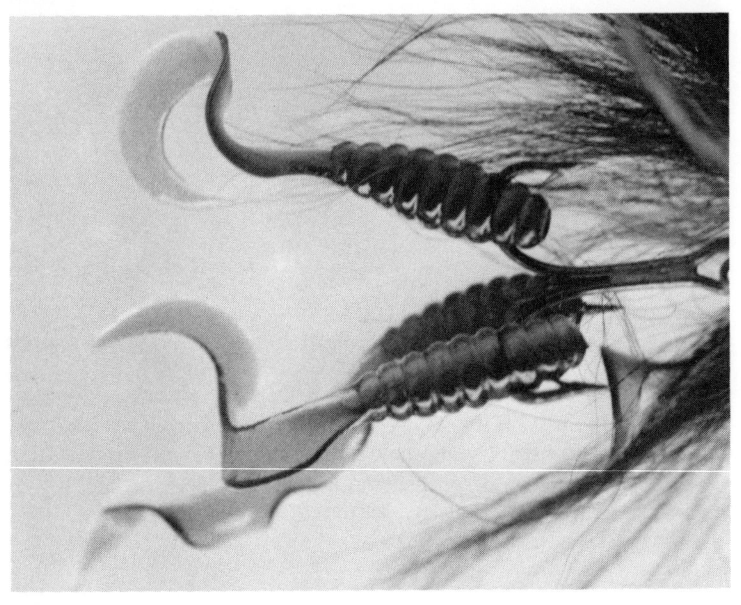

To add a little rubber to the back of your bucktails, just hook them on as shown. In the water it helps slow the lure down by increasing water resistance and adds a lot of extra action. Two to six inch grubs or rubber worms can be added with equal success.

Clear fingernail polish does wonders when applied to the wrappings of a bucktail to protect them from the razor sharp teeth of the pike. In many pike infested lakes where anglers catch twenty or more fish in a day, this practice of coating the wrappings will extend the life of the lure by three or four times.

Jigs for Pike Fishing

One group of lures which is often overlooked by anglers is the use of jigs as a lure to catch northern pike. At certain times of the year the jig is by far the easiest and most effective lure to catch northern pike. The jig consists of a hook with a piece of lead attached to the shank. Hair or rubber is added to the hook to make it resemble some kind of baitfish.

The weight of jig used is in direct proportion to the depth of water you are in. To fish a jig properly, first select a jig that will work well at the depth needed, then make modifications from there.

1/8 ounce	two to six feet
1/4 ounce	six to twelve feet
1/2 ounce	twelve to twenty feet
3/4 ounce	twenty to thirty-two feet
1 ounce	thirty-two to forty-five feet

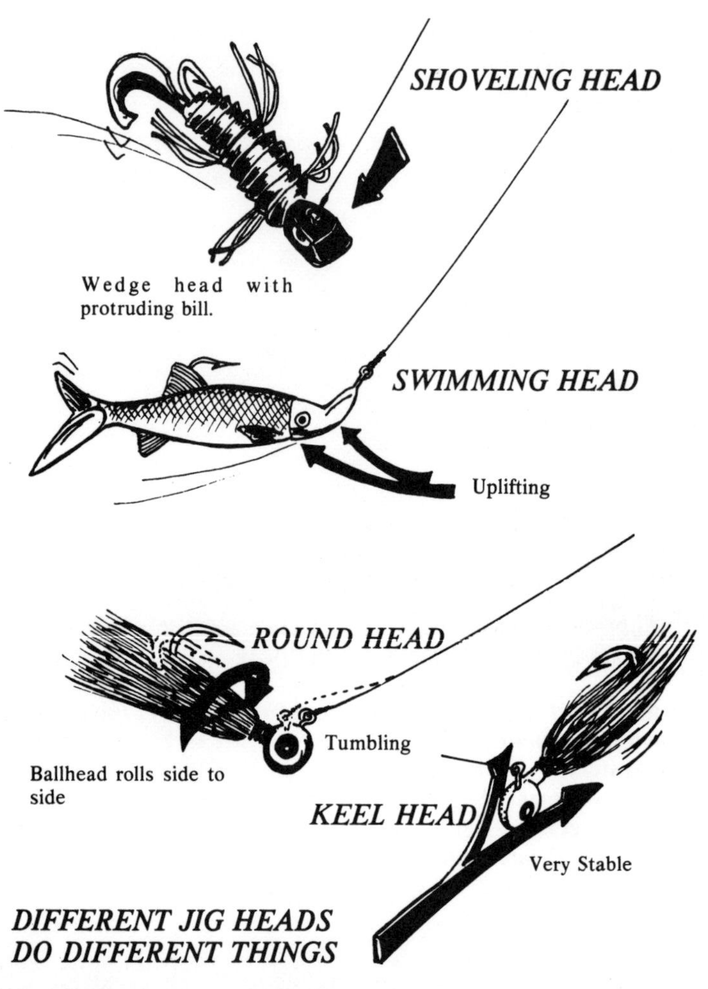

When selecting the type of jig shape to buy, keep in mind how you intend to use it. The round and keel headed shapes are best for fishing under the boat and the shoveling or swimming head shapes are best for casting.

The dressings added to a jig are best when they contain very bright colors like silver tinsel. This extra amount of flash drives the pike crazy. White, silver and yellow are the three jig colors which seem to have the best success overall.Often minnows are added to the jig to make them more effective. When this is done, there may not even be a need to use any hair or rubber on your jig to make them productive. Since the northern is such a hard striking fish, it is only on a rare occasion while fishing jigs will live bait be needed to get a strike. Jigs are commonly used in areas where the bottom contour drops very fast into deep water and there is a need to stay tight to the bottom. Jigs can be fished by casting, trolling or drifting and is one of the most underrated pike lures around.

Wire leaders are again a must when gearing up to catch pike, especially with jigs. A solid strand of stainless steel wire is the best way to protect the main line from being cut. (see photo)

One good tip for protecting jigs from bite-offs without using any distracting snaps or swivels would be the use of a single strand of stainless steel wire. Simply thread the wire through eye of the jig and twist several times. This protective wire need not be more than nine inches in length and can be attached quickly and securely to a jig or plug with excellent results.

Lure Storage

With so many different lures being used to catch pike, anglers have the obvious problem of how to properly store larger baits. The safest and driest way to protect your lures is to buy a box, or a series of boxes that can hold your larger baits. Rather than buying a tackle box the size of a refrigerator, look to buy one of the new boxes styled like a small suit case that come with compartments on one or both sides. These boxes are designed with only one deep compartment and are built so the length of any lure will fit inside.

For the folks who wish to cut some corners, an old ice chest maybe modified to hold your baits by drilling a series of holes around the outside rim. Your lures can then hang down into the chest free from major tangles.

Big pike baits are often stored in foam coolers to help keep them dry and at least semi-organized. A hole should be placed in the bottom to permit water to drain out.

The large hooks found on many good pike baits must be respected at all times, spending a little extra time trying to keep the inside of the boat organized is a great practice. Expensive lures can quickly fall victim to rust and mutilation if not stored properly.

Sharpening Hooks

This is an appropriate time to talk about getting and keeping the hooks sharp as a razor on all lures and rigs. Even if the lure just came out of the package, steps must be taken to re-sharpen each hook and keep them sharp, too. The bigger and older pike become, the tougher their mouth becomes and the harder it is to get the hook to penetrate the already boney jaw of a pike.

The procedure for sharpening a hook is actually quite simple. A fine jeweler's file or soft stone is needed. Working only the outside tip of the hook with steady strokes in only the direction of the hook's eye, the point should sharpen up with only a few quick strokes. One little tip to see if the hook is sharp enough would be to see if it can easily scratch your fingernail. Every hook should be tested in this manner before it is attached to the line. Anglers are reminded to periodically check their hooks while fishing to make sure they stay razor sharp. Rocks, stumps and weeds can all cause the tips of your hooks to go dull.(see photo)

Having and keeping your hooks sharp is one step everyone can take to increase their overall success during a season. It may mean only one or two more fish this season, but what happens if one of those fish turns out to be thirty pounds?

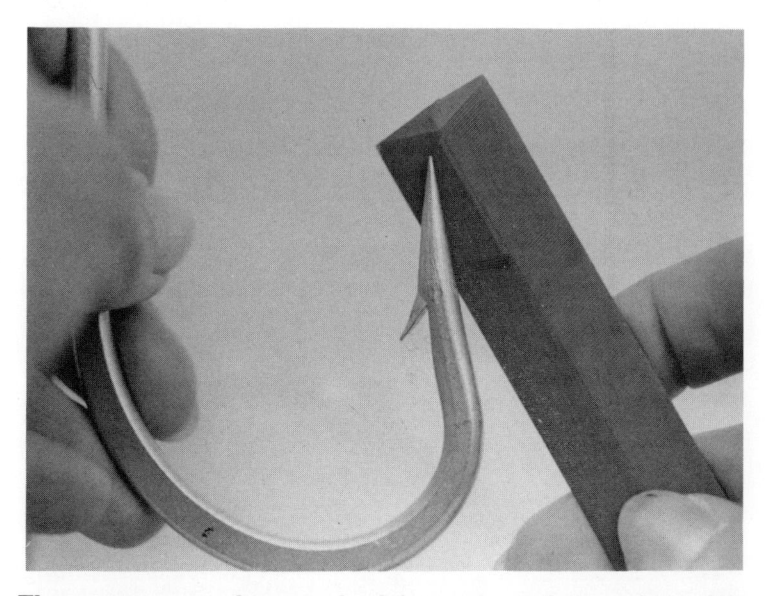

The proper way to sharpen a hook is to only work the outside of the point with short sweeps toward the eye of the hook. It is good to get into the practice of sharpening every hook in the tackle box to increase the odds of a good hookset.

CHAPTER SIX

Live and Dead Bait Rigs

Of the three senses the northern pike uses to feed, sight, sound and smell each can be used by the pike when it is to their advantage. The smell sense is what makes the difference in angling success for pike when conditions are tough. Live and dead bait angling methods of Europe are far ahead of those used in America. A vast majority of the anglers in the United States and Canada continue to fish pike rain or shine with artificial lures. This has proven to be a major downfall to consistent angling success because many fishermen simply look down at anglers who fish with bait.

For people looking to improve their success at pike angling at all times of the year, bait fishing methods simply **MUST** be used. Contrary to what many people would like to think about pike, they have a well developed sense of smell that is often used to guide them to their prey. It is easy to envision pike springing out from behind a clump of weed to gobble down some unsuspecting baitfish. The truth of the matter is pike would prefer taking the easiest meal they can find even if it is already dead! This is why with some bait fishing techniques a dead minnow is used with fantastic success.

The forms of live baits used often include the hearty sucker minnow which can be transported and kept alive better than any other type of live minnow. Large shiner minnows are another popular form of live. The silver shiner is very difficult to

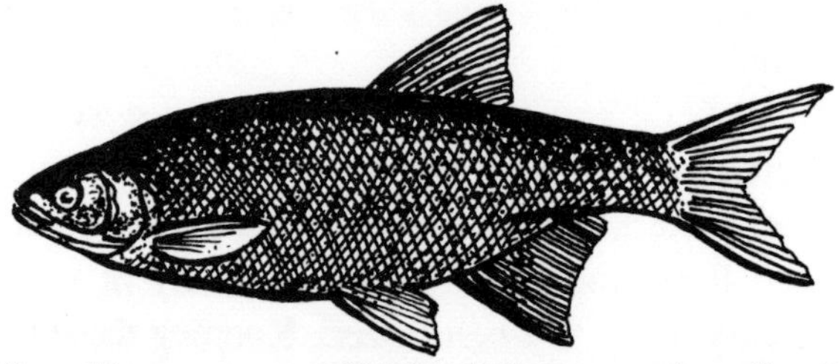

Large golden shiners are an effective baits to use for pike. Lots of fresh water and no more than six shiners per bucket can keep these fragile, but effective baits alive. Shiners six to ten inches in length are the sizes most readily available.

keep alive, but the golden shiner is much tougher and is used by most pike anglers. The sizes most often used are suckers or shiners about six inches long. In areas where trophy fish can exist, live minnows up to a pound have been used successfully.

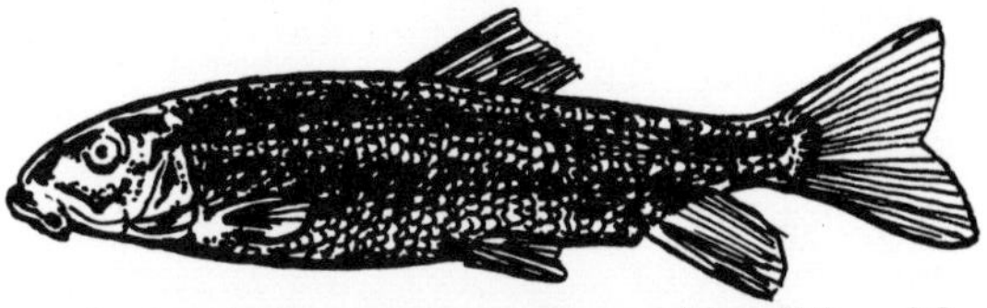

The sucker minnow is the most popular and traditional form of pike bait. Used with both live and dead bait methods, the sucker is the heartiest and most readily available of all the "pike" minnows. The most effective sizes are six to ten inches in length.

Minnow buckets come in all different shapes and designs.During the colder months of the year, a foam bucket will do a fine job of keeping the minnows alive, but during the summer, a bucket that can be submerged into the water is a easier way of getting fresh water to the minnows. The warmer the water, the more oxygen their bodies will demand.

As with artificial lures, the size of bait you select does have a way of effecting the odds of catching quantity or quality fish. Dead baits include smelt or small herring. These baits are best purchased fresh and packaged individually in wax paper so they are easy to get at when frozen. Keeping these baits frozen until they actually hit the water is the only way to properly use them. Both smelt and herring turn to a clump of mush as soon as they thaw. Dead baits do not last long when they are put on a hook, but then again, this is what probably makes them so effective. The strong "fishy" odor given off by these two fish do exactly what anglers hope to do, attract a big pike by scent!

Bait rigs come in many different versions, many of which are one of a kind, custom tied or built for a special purpose. In traveling around the country, some areas would use one rig almost exclusively while fifty miles away, anglers use a completely different style of bait fishing.

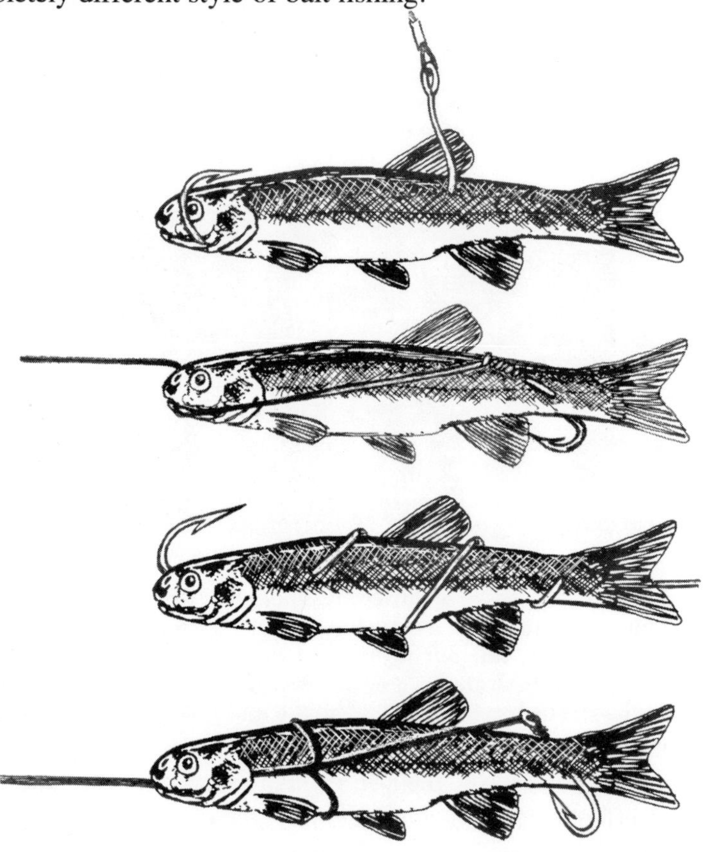

Securing a hook in a dead bait rig can be accomplished with a wide combination of hooking procedures, above are just a few of the ways baitfish can be attached to a dead bait rig. The main reason some baits are threaded or wrapped when adding hooks is to simply keep the soft fragile bodies of the baitfish from tearing off the hook while casting.

Bait rigging for pike consists of three basic concepts and the countless variations used to custom fit a rig to a particular lake or region. First there are the simple bottom rigs, they are designed to be used mostly with dead baits. Next we have the suspended rigs, used most often with a bobber and live bait. Third, we have the strip-on rigs, which combine the use of bait with spinners or jigs.

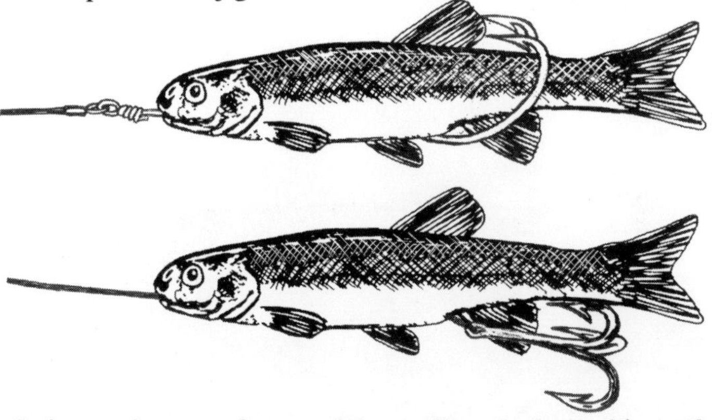

Strip-on rigs are often used by trollers, because this method of hooking a baitfish will permit the bait to be used for trolling without twisting or tangling your line as it is pulled through the water.

Bottom rigs are designed to be simply cast out from shore or boat and permitted to sink to the bottom with little or no extra weight to help keep the bait down. They consist of a single large hook with maybe one small treble hook attached to a short length of wire. Depending on how deep you plan to fish will control the need for sinkers to help keep the baits near the bottom.

Suspended bait rigs often use a special dead bait hook or a large single hook. The key to the success of these rigs is to suspend the bait at a depth used by the pike. A bobber is used to suspend the bait above the bottom or weeds. It is important to place all sinkers about 18 inches above the hook to permit the minnow a little freedom and to give the feeding fish time to grab the bait without feeling any resistance. Enough sinkers should be added to the line so the bobber you select is only submerged halfway, to permit the least amount of extra resistance when a pike moves off with the bait. Bobbers can range in style from the old fashion wooden type that you manually set at the depth you will be fishing, to the newer sliding bobber rigs that can make fishing pike with a bobber effective at any depth.

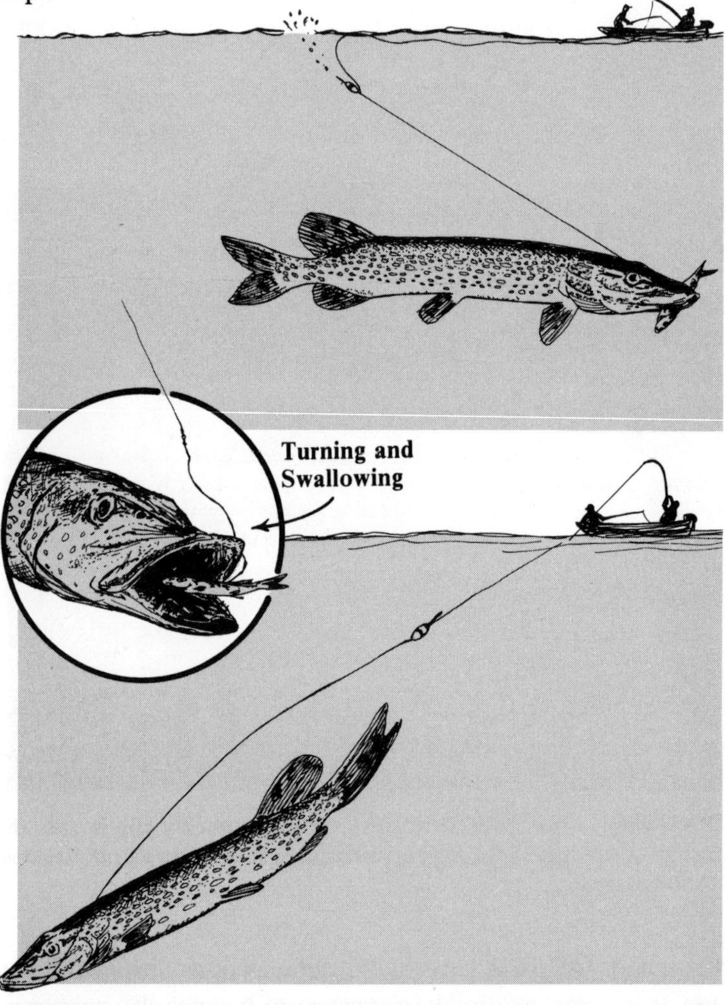

When a pike strikes a suspended rig, the bobber is used to gage when the pike has the bait completely swallowed. A standard rule to use is to set the hook when the pike makes his second run. A hook should never be set until the pike is moving away from the angler for a better angle in setting the hooks.

A sliding bobber rig is different than just a bobber attached to the line. It often takes a special bobber with either a hole or straw running right through it or a fine slit that the line can be inserted into and a special clip on both ends of the bobber keep it in place. With a sliding bobber rig, the first thing that is put on the line is a bobber stop of some sort. Most anglers simply use a piece of nylon fishing line and tie a small knot around their fishing line. With a little effort, the knot can be slid up and down the main line. The bobber is now attached to the line and it will freely slide up and down until it reaches the knot.

This sliding bobber will permit the angler to quickly clip it onto the line. Note the small piece of braided fishing line tied in a knot to act as a bobber stop.

The rest of the rig is exactly the same as other suspended bait rigs. It is again extremely important to balance the bobber so that it will sink just below the halfway mark on the bobber. The small knot is now set at whatever depth you need and instead of standing on your toes to get the bobber and minnow out from shore, the bobber and sinkers slide close together for easy casting. When this compact rig hits the water the line will be pulled through the bobber and stop at the depth you have pre-set. The sliding bobber rigs make it possible for anglers to fish at any depth.

Other than the plain hook and line system of bait fishing, anglers can also use bait with spinners in what is commonly called a strip-on rig. Minnows, mostly small suckers, are threaded onto a pre-made harness that will use a double or treble hook secured to the rear of the minnow. Strip-on spinner rigs are the most effective when trolled or drifted, but due to the fact that the minnow can easily be torn, casting with these rigs is not a very good idea.

Dressing a jig with a minnow is commonly used by many walleye anglers. This method of bait fishing is a real favorite among many anglers. The minnow is attached to the hook in one of three ways. By hooking the minnow through the lips, it is permitted to swim along with the jig and if a very slow method of fishing is used, this can be very effective. When the minnow is being cast or fished very quickly, as when fishing above a weedbed, insert the hook in the minnows mouth and out the back of his head. This is the best way to hook the minnow to prevent it from coming off the hook while casting.

The use of a plain jig head dressed with a minnow can be extremely effective on pike as well as walleye.This method of hooking the minnow allows the angler a greater chance to cast the bait without losing it.

For drifting slowly, or still fishing, the minnow can be hooked through the dorsal fin and permitted to swim freely.

The selection of hook size with any of the bait rigs is a very important factor in the success ratio of strikes to landed fish. Too large of a hook and the fish will have a hard time swallowing the bait, too small and it is very difficult to get the hook into the fish at all. The rule to follow when selecting the proper hook size is to make sure the gap of the hook is at least as wide as the minnow is across the back.

When treble hooks are used, anglers can get by with a #6 or #4 hook with almost any size bait because more than one of these hooks is used on any one minnow and their three barbed attack gives excellent results.

In states where more than one hook is prohibited on a plain line, anglers are reminded to add a simple bead or maybe a small spinner just ahead of the hooks which will then make the bait rig into a lure, thus becoming legal to have more than one hook on the rig.

Hooking your Baits

The way in which the minnow is attached to the hook is a very critical step, from the standpoint of hooking power and placement without damaging a lively minnow. The diagrams that follow graphically show the best locations to place hooks, but it is extremely important to consider how the bait will be fished **BEFORE** a minnow is even hooked!

When still fishing or fishing directly over the bait, hooking the minnow in the dorsal fin area is preferred. When trolling or casting a minnow and it will be moving at all times, hook the minnow so it will swim naturally through the water by hooking it in the nose or lips. When adding a minnow to a harness or other type of rig where a minnow can be alive or dead, be sure to keep the body of the minnow as straight as possible, because as the bent minnow is pulled through the water, it will spin and twist your line.

For still fishing or very slow drifting, hooking the minnow through the dorsal fin as shown above can be done. This is a very popular method of hooking minnows, but with suckers it is wise to place the hook just under the dorsal fin so the hook will not tear out of the suckers body when being cast out or pulled through weeds.

Often when the pike are in a finicky mood, hooking the minnow so that the hookpoints towardthe head of the bait will give some outstanding results. This method of hooking minnows is especially popular during the winter months for hooking dead bait rigs. It is critical when dead baits are used to make sure they are suspended parallel to the bottom.This makes it easier for the pike to grab, and seems more natural.

While trolling, drifting or even limited casting, the hooking of the minnow through the lips will help avoid line twist and keep the minnow lively.

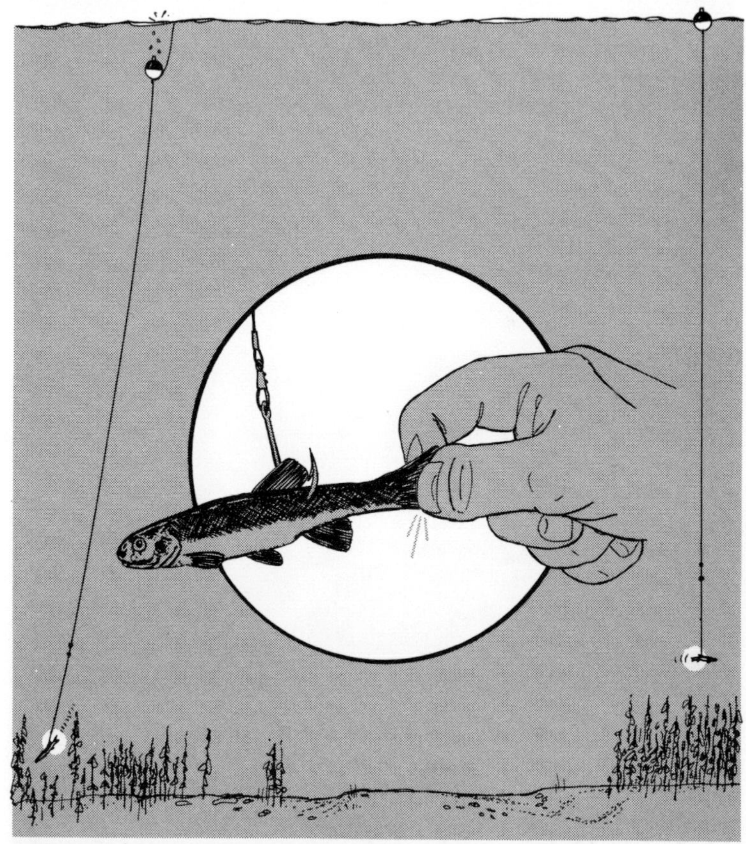

When the sucker minnow becomes a little too aggressive, one tip would be too simply pinch off or cut off a portion of the minnows tail. This will make it possible for the sucker to still wiggle like crazy, but not go anywhere! Many also believe that roughing up the sides of the sucker with a knife makes the suckers body give off more scent to attract a hungry pike.

Making Wire Snells

Braided copper or stainless steel wire is used for live bait rigs because they are very flexible and do not easily kink. Coated wire is also popular if more than one hook is to be added to the rig. By making just a few twists of the coated wire, the hook can be locked permanently into position with the heat of a match. Many of the bait rigs shown here are "home made" simply because the lack of commercially tied rigs are not readily available. Many of the rigs must be custom fitted for the size and type of baits used. With a little practice, making your own live bait rigs will not only prove to be more reliable than commercially made rigs, but they can save you money too!

CHAPTER SEVEN

Seasonal Pike Fishing Techniques

The selection of the proper fishing methods for catching a big pike is not always an exacting procedure that can be written here in black and white. A countless number of uncontrollable factors can effect how a situation is fished successfully. Understanding the challenge in fishing, is part of what makes a day out on the water so intriguing. It has already been mentioned that firsthand experience is the only true way to become a better pike angler, but this next section of the book should provide some new insight into the wide variety of techniques used in fishing for pike today.

If there is one common problem among anglers all across the world, it would be their blinding confidence in "traditional" methods of fishing. An open mind in fishing makes it possible to catch fish from places other people never fish, with lures or methods other anglers may have never seen before. Having and keeping an open mind is the edge fishermen must develop if they ever hope to be a true master of the sport.

Spring Pike Fishing

Throughout much of the northern pike's range, special legislation has been created to protect this great fish from being taken while spawning is taking place. Big pike often group together in large numbers and anglers knowing this can take advantage of this situation. Many people believe taking a number of big fish before they spawn would be harmful to the lake or river over the course of several years. The pre-spawn feeding activity of pike is often quite good, but seasonal restrictions in most areas make fishing for them at this time against the law.

The states of North and South Dakota have one of the prime northern pike waters in the United States where the season does not close. Every spring, many of the avid pike anglers head to the expansive Missouri River System to take advantage of some outstanding action.

Earlier in the book a point was made that the two peak grow-

Anglers of all ages love to catch northern pike. The secret to catching a nice stringer like this is finding a system or area producing fish and stick to it. Try to understand not only where the pike came from, but why they are there. This could set up a "pattern" for finding pike in other areas on the same lake.

ing seasons of the pike took place in early spring, and again in late summer. These two peak growing seasons also turn out to be the two prime times to be catching some big female pike! On the Missouri River System of Lake Oahe, the peak feeding spree takes place at the end of March. Northern pike move into the shallow muddy bays where warm waters have attracted large groups of baitfish. When the action peaks, large silver

Rapala type baits cast into only a few feet of water can be a very productive way to fish. In North Dakota, on Lake Sakakawea, the pike begin to concentrate in large numbers while the main lake is still frozen. The best action will occur here the first two weeks after the ice leaves the main lake. Pike are again found in the back sides of shallow bays, but dead bait methods rather than artificials catch 95 percent of the pike.

If for some reason the spring weather has been cool, the pike still go on feed, but not in large groups. This makes angling with artificial lures very challenging. Dead smelt are the most consistent bait for catching pike at this time of year. Shore fishermen do a great job with bottom rigs, and some use bobbers when fishing from boats. Big pike often suspend just under the surface around the mouths of those shallow muddy bottom bays to let the sunlight warm their bodies and help mature the eggs faster.

Action at this time of year is often very hot or cold. The nicer the weather, the quicker the action peaks and falls off. When the big pike begin hanging around possible feeding and spawning areas, they are worse than the stock market for predicting when they will be active or when you might just as well stay home.

Fishermen in other areas where pike fishing is legal all year should spend most of their time fishing the area just outside the spawning grounds of the pike. The largest pike in any lake or river system are the last to come up and spawn. By fishing the outside edges of the spawning area with dead bait tactics, anglers will find some outstanding fishing.

Remember, no matter where you fish for the best and most consistent pre-spawn pike action, the dead bait methods of bottom fishing or suspended rig fishing are the most productive. Heavy females will not want to work any harder than they absolutely need to in order to feed, so anglers must fish slow and cautiously at all times for best success.

By the time most of the prime northern pike waters regulated by fishing seasons are open, the pike are in a post-spawn con-

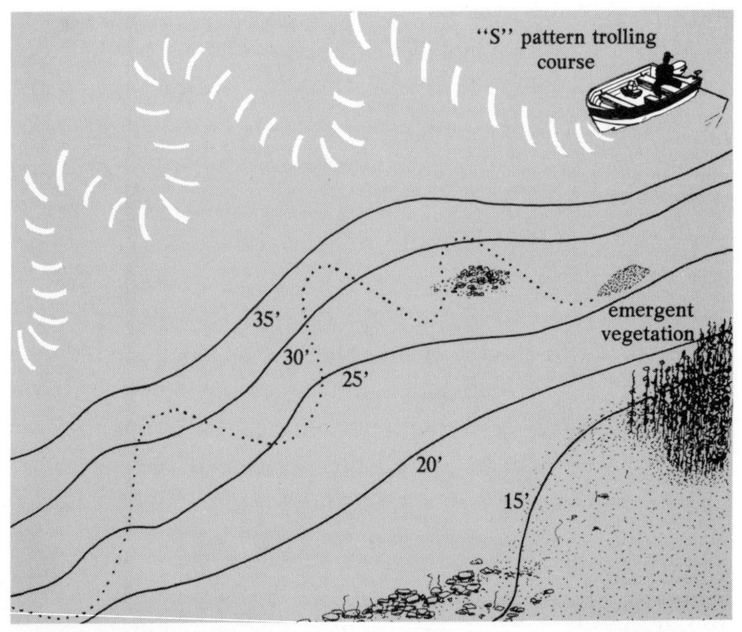

When working springtime pike, it is often wise to use an "S" pattern to your slower trolling passes. This will make it easier to locate the depth used most often by pike. the prime ares would be near river inlets, emergent vegetation and outside known spawning areas.

dition. This term means they have spawned and are now getting ready for summer. Opening day is often a great event in many states, and although the walleye receives much of the attention, the northern pike action can be excellent as long as fishermen understand where and how to fish them.

After spawning has been completed, the pike are in no real hurry to leave the area near the spawning sights. Female pike often move to deeper water and simply rest. The movement to deeper water will occur for both mature males and females, with the males being the last to leave the spawning areas. The smaller immature pike are what many walleye anglers encounter while out fishing. These small pike hit anything that moves and can become quite a problem on some lakes. Frustrated fishermen often use names like, slim, toothy, snake or hammerhandles to describe smaller pike.

My first experience with opening day pike occurred when

business kept me in town for the biggest fishing weekend of the season. My family decided to make a one day trip to a local fishing lake which was known to have a walleyes. As usual, the lake was simply alive with anglers, both on shore and in

Spring walleye anglers often run into a pleasant surprise when they move to deeper water. The jig and minnow combination so effective with walleyes can be equally effective on pike.

boats. Fishing action was poor in areas where fishermen had hoped to catch walleye, so my attention was steered to northerns. Knowing that a large marshy bay with a small creek flowing into it would be a prime pike spawning area for the lake, our party began fishing with many of the more traditional methods of trolling and casting spoons in the shallow waters just outside the rushes that lined the lakes shore.

When spoons and spinnerbaits were used, only a few hammer handle size pike were taken. Looking as though the opener was going to be one of the worst ever, we did the only logical thing, had lunch! We stopped the boat right in the middle of the bay and opened a bucket of chicken. When lunch was over, the boat had drifted out the mouth of the bay and was headed out to the main lake. Since everyone was not quite ready to begin fishing again, a 1/4 ounce walleye jig and minnow combination was dropped to the bottom as we drifted along. It wasn't long before a pike snapped off the jig, which was directly attached to ten pound line without a leader. Since the action that day was poor, any sign of fish life was an occasion to notice. A new jig was quickly added to the line, but this time with a wire leader. Within short order, a beautiful seven pound pike was landed. This fish came from 24 feet of water! Before the day was out, the entire group had a limit of pike from five to fourteen pounds taken from water between 20 and 40 feet!

To this day, the experience of that one trip has made for many other successful outings. It is a perfect example of how the pike move out and rest in deeper water after spawning has been completed.

Dead bait tactics on post-spawn northern pike have worked in the same type of areas by my family taking fish up to twenty four pounds! The jig and minnow combination is one of the most enjoyable ways to catch pike when they are found in deep water. The secret is to simply work the first major drop-off to deep water outside the spawning area. Since in early spring the water has not yet thermoclined, the pike are more free to roam to any depth where the water temperature and light conditions are just right for them. In some lakes this grouping of pike may take place in fifteen feet of water while on another just across the road the pike look for fifty feet.

This obvious and deliberate move to deeper water explains why walleye anglers do not catch many pike. The majority of walleye fishing at this time of year is done in twelve feet of water or less.

This period of rest after spawning lasts for no longer than three weeks. As soon as they feel like feeding, they move shallow again and feed like crazy! This frenzy happens almost every year at the same time on the Mississippi River near Wabasha Minnesota. In the backwaters of the river, the pike move to the shallow flats and feed heavily on the smaller fish looking for food around last year's vegetation. Starting about the third week in May in southern Minnesota, this frenzy sweeps the lakes further north in a very short period of time after that. In other areas, look for the pike to be grouped in old weed beds or ones just starting to grow.

Spring pike often move to river mouths to feed after they have recovered from spawning. The spawning sucker minnow is the reason pike move to these areas. Where ever the suckers go, the big pike will be right behind them. Anglers can often find large pike in only a few feet of water at this time of year and is one of the few times topwater baits would be a good choice for pike fishing.

Spring conditions travel north at a rate of 15 miles per day. If the pike start feeding heavily in a lake 100 miles south, the fish should be active in your area in about ten days. This does not take into account the varying water temperatures in shallow or deep lakes. The intensity of this feeding movement relies heavily on the spawn taking place over a short period of time while groups of post-spawn pike in a lake or river will still be together. With cold or unusual weather patterns taking place during the spawn, the pike will drag out the total time pike will be in an area, because some will still be recovering from spawning and others will have spawned and be long gone.

Angling methods will involve any method of fishing that can be done successfully in shallow weed infested areas. This will include the use of spinnerbaits, crankbaits, bucktails, topwater lures and spoons. Bait fishing methods will work well too, but since these pike will literally hit anything that moves, artificial lures are often easiest to use.

This post-spawn activity will be the last major grouping of big pike the lake will see until the end of summer. For anglers lucky enough to be on the water when the pike start their feeding frenzy, ENJOY IT! Because big and small pike alike go crazy for no longer than a week.

By the first of June, northern pike begin to relocate in areas on the lake or river where they can find food, security and comfort. Pike are one of the first fish to get into their summer feeding patterns. Studies have shown some pike prefer not to stray far from a kind of "home" territory, while others prefer to roam all across the lake. This makes it difficult from a fisherman's standpoint to give yes and no answers to where all the bigger pike would be.

The truth of the matter is that after the post-spawn feeding frenzy, the bigger pike become very hard to find. Pike fishing in general is often very good, but success with larger fish seems to drop off steadily as the summer progresses.

It is a widely held belief that a vast majority of the big pike in a lake go deep and since they are much deeper than most anglers normally fish, success must drop off. New research done with radio tracking devices show that northern pike do go deeper, but not excessively deep to account for poor angling success. This research seems to support the theory that the pike are often in or very near areas where fishermen frequent, but have gone into a non-feeding stage. The older the pike become, the more time they spend "resting".

The pike or "water wolf" has an international reputation for being a fish that eats anything that moves, so how can a creature like this just shut off its habit of eat, eat, eat? The answer again seems to support the resting pike theory, as adult pike have the unique capability of living for weeks on no food at all.

It is very possible that both theories of why the big pike seem to disappear as summer approaches have some merit. The large pike often seek out the cooler deep water areas on a lake to rest, where their bodies will demand little food.

Having spent a great deal of fishing time in areas known to have big northern pike, only rarely do these elusive trophies show themselves. The pike's cousin the muskie is one fish that can be found and caught in deep water, but deep water action for the really big pike is very rare.

The puzzle of taking big pike all summer long has many possibilities, but to date no definite fishing pattern has been found. Anglers are then steered into fishing for the smaller pike from one to five pounds. Not to say big pike should be forgotten totally during late spring and most of the summer, but the odds of scoring on bigger pike can be slim. This time of year is often a common time to take a weeks vacation. Guides, who make their living putting people on fish, often use the aggressive feeding habits of the smaller pike to their advantage. No matter what the weather or time of day, it would seem that the younger northern pike are always willing to bite. Knowing that a three pound pike can fight like a wildcat, can offer a great sporting challenge for fishermen using light tackle.

These smaller pike can be quick to strike and are often found nearly everywhere an angler wets a line. "Hammerhandle" size pike will strike a panfish lure with the same vigor as a large spoon. This is probably the reason northern pike have such little respect among purist muskie, walleye, bass or panfish lovers. The smaller "pesty" northerns can make a nuisance of itself, but a day on the water without at least a few pike to keep things exciting could get very dull.

Summertime Fishing Tactics

As the waters warm, angling techniques for pike angling become more and more deep water orientated. The term "deep water" is relative to each lake. The weedline edge where they stop growing is the beginning of the "deep water" on that particular lake. Jig fishing with or without live bait added now becomes very productive. Live baits to do a noticeably better job of attracting pike than the dead baits that were so effective early in the season. A very noticeable preference for dawn and dusk feeding also takes hold, especially for the bigger fish.

Spring fed lakes and rivers can be the exceptions for a slump in summertime big pike action. The areas on the lake where the springs actually enter the lake form the "ideal" temperatures and conditions in many cases for pike to hold all summer. When this occasion comes up, standard spring tactics of dead bait fishing can be extremely effective. Pike tend to group in these areas very closely, so bait fishing methods have proven to be the most effective once the "honey hole" is found. A large spring area is often not much larger than the size of an average car!

An excellent oxygen supply and ideal water temperatures make it possible for the pike to use these areas when they occur at any depth. It is very difficult for the average fisherman to detect a spring in deep water. When springs are flowing into a lake in a shallow portion of the lake or river, you can find them by checking surface water temperatures with an electronic temperature probe to get instant readings. One could also spend a little less money and simply put your hand over the side of the boat to detect any temperature change. Pike relating to springs will often group closely together. To be successful, it is ex-

Digital water temperature devices can aid anglers in finding under water springs that may hold pike all summer long.It is best to look for such places on a calm day, because wave action can mix-up the water making it hard to find the exact location.

tremely important that enough time be spent to pin-point the exact location of the spring before fishing.

If you own a home or cabin near a lake, it is often possible to visually spot areas where springs occur. The constant flow of a spring has the same water temperature summer and winter, so as the lake tries to freeze in the winter, the area above the spring is the last to freeze if it freezes at all! By simply noting where these open areas are on the lake, the location of a spring can be easily found during the open water season.

Fishing the springs on a lake can offer exceptional fishing for big fish when other areas draw a blank. This could be one answer to catching big pike all summer long on some lakes and rivers.

Speed Trolling for Pike

One of the advantages of fishing the warmer waters of summer is the use of the speed trolling technique to catch pike. Just as the name implies, speed trolling involves trolling at a very fast pace. The whole idea of this fishing method is to appeal to the pike's instinct to strike. Using the senses of sight and sound, the pike are quickly exposed to a fast moving lure. The pike respond without thinking to quickly strike at the lure. Speed trolling or "spoonplugging," as it is also called, is one of those methods many have to see work before they believe. First time speed trollers are often amazed by this unique fishing method made popular by Buck Perry, commonly referred to as the "father of structure fishing." Mr. Perry has used his method of spoonplugging to catch fish of all kinds all across the country. He designed the spoonplug, which is a lure built to travel at high speeds without twisting or running out of tune.

Water temperature is one of the most important keys to successful speed trolling, because if the water falls below 65 degrees, the metabolism of a northern pike just can not seem to react quick enough to a fast moving lure.

How fast is fast? The trolling speed selected should never be permanently set at only one speed. This is commonly misunderstood by anglers thinking "speed trolling" must be trolling at twenty miles an hour. A fast jogging pace is usually the average trolling rate. Changing boat speed until fish are found is simply a wise practice to remember when trolling for any species.

Boat control while speed trolling involves only straight line trolling passes over an area. In recent years many fishermen have grown aware of the "edges" or places where the lake's contours drop rapidly into deep water. Fish of all sorts love to frequent these areas, so trolling along the edge close to the break is a good bet. Speed trollers often cannot control the boat at high speeds to follow the unpredictable shapes of the lake bottom, thus straight line trolling passes are required. More simply put, anglers should make a series of 100 yard trolling passes back and forth over an area to systematically cover the entire area.

To saturate an area properly, begin the first trolling passes in

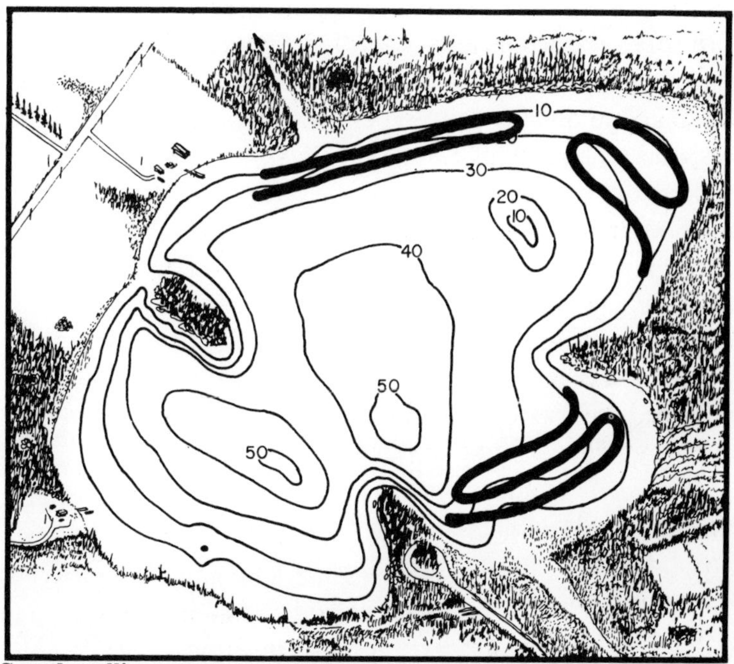

Speed trolling passes are made with a series of short straight line passes working from shallow to deep.

water ten feet deep or less. Systematically troll deeper and deeper until fish are caught. With this shallow to deep system, lure selection must be made to correspond with depth you wish to fish. The spoonplug is a very popular lure to use for this fishing technique and a complete size selection of these lures is available for exactly this purpose. Other lures like the Hellbender, Mudbug and others with metal lips perform very well at high speeds and also come in a wide variety of sizes to accommodate various depths.

Lure color for this method of trolling is not a major factor in your success since the fish simply hit these lures out of impulse. Occasionally there maybe a need to stop and cast an area, so the speed trolling lures can also double as deep running crankbaits. Lures made with the bright metallic colors of silver and brass are good choices.

Twelve to twenty pound monofilament is most commonly used for this kind of trolling. Lines with low stretch factors are preferred as lure vibrations are more easily transmitted through

Two popular and effective spoonplugging lures are the Hellbender (left) and the Spoonplug itself. The secret to the success of these lures is their ability to travel very fast through the water without rolling or running out of tune.

low stretch line. Knowing if the lure is running free of weeds along with knowing when it bumps the bottom can be hard to detect with a stretchy line which quickly absorbs any vibrations the lure may make.

The heavier the line test used, the more water resistance is created by the diameter of the line. This makes it more difficult for the lure to reach bottom, because the bow in the line acts like a parachute for the lure. In most cases, twelve and fourteen pound test Stren line will work well for this kind of fishing. However, anglers must take note of any nicks or scrapes on the line that could have been made while the lure bounced off the bottom. Wire line has been a real secret for anglers wanting to get their lures down deep. Solid strand 18 pound stainless steel line is ideal for this purpose, but special care must be taken not to kink this line.

The key to catching more than one pike from an area while speed trolling is to duplicate your exact speed and depth along with knowing exactly how far behind the boat the lure was running. This can be easily done by marking the line in some way to be aware of exactly how much line was out when the last fish struck. A waterproof magic marker does this very well and will not damage your line in any way.

LINE BOW CREATED BY WATER RESISTANCE

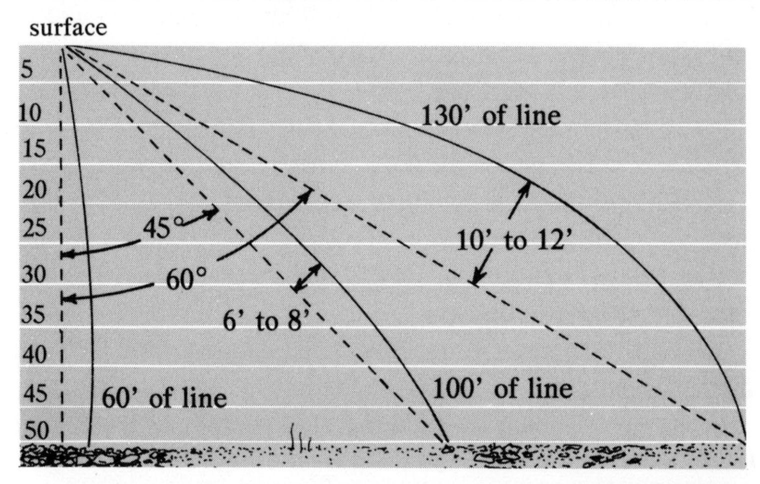

As any lure or bait is pulled through the water, a constant force is put on the line. This resistance forms a bow in the line which is another form of slack line. This extra amount of slack can hurt your hooksetting power and decrease your sensitivity in detecting the bottom or a strike. The thicker the line diameter, the more resistance the water will put on it. Water resistance can also act like a parachute to prohibit some lures from reaching the bottom.

Boat speed is one factor many anglers do by feel, but a trolling speed indicator is by far the best way of insuring consistent speeds. These are simple devices that register how much water resistance is created as the boat moves through the water. There are many commercially made types as well as many homemade models. There is no preference for style or make, anything that will assist in giving a more consistent speed will be a big asset in your fishing success.

A short stiff muskie type rod is ideal for this method of fast trolling. The constant resistance to pull the lures through the water will put undue strain on a soft action rod and could break.

The bait casting reels do a fine job of holding the heavier lines used for speed trolling, but in many cases, they are simply too high class! The less expensive trolling reels that cost about one fourth of what you might pay for a good bait casting reel are ideal for trolling. The higher quality baitcasting reels are simply an over kill in equipment selection. The basic function of holding line and cranking in your lure is done very nicely with the less expensive trolling reels and the money you save can be then spent on more lures!

Wire leaders are very seldom used by veteran speed trollers. The faster rate at which the lures move through the water make it difficult for the teeth of a pike to touch the line. Leaders also tend to collect weeds that can cause poor fishing success. Heavy duty snaps are commonly used to make quick changes in lure size as the depth increases.

One cardinal rule for trolling which anglers should watch for is the problem of weeds on the lure. A good troller periodically checks the lure to make sure everything is running clean. Each time before a new lure is dropped behind the boat, it is wise to run the lure along side the boat for a short distance to make sure it is running properly at the speed in which the boat is traveling. Tuning a plug to run straight only takes a few seconds with the aid of a long nose pair of pliers. (see diagram)

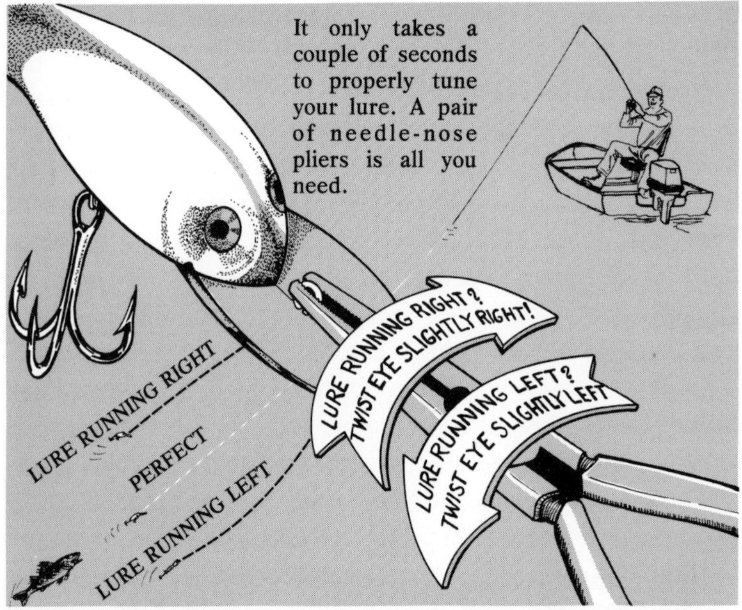

Plugs or "crankbaits" often need a little fine-tuning to insure they will run straight. It is wise to tune every lure before you start fishing to make sure it is giving you the proper action.

Since a great majority of the summer pike fishing action will take place near drop-offs, anglers can also do well casting lures in these areas. Deep diving crankbaits would be the best bet to cast shallow and bring down the break. The long thin plugs are popular, but many bass anglers will admit that the pike also love the short chunky crankbaits as well.

Since a great majority of the summer pike fishing action will take place near drop-offs, anglers can also do well casting lures in these areas. Deep diving crankbaits would be the best bet to cast shallow and bring down the break. The long thin plugs are popular, but many bass anglers will admit that the pike also love the short chunky crankbaits as well.

Weed edges are often "hotspots" for pike anglers, especially when they are located near deep water. Isolated weed clumps near points and rivers flowing into a lake are ideal areas for anglers who prefer to bait fish from an anchored boat rather than casting or trolling. The key ingredient for anglers looking to fish from an anchored position is to select a unique area in which to fish that differs from the surrounding area. Anglers dropping anchor in just any old spot and hoping the pike will come to them are short sighted, because the really big pike like to make a home in the most ideal locations on the lake. It pays to purchase an electronic depth finder and use it to explore the lake or river to find the unique places that may be holding pike.

The secret to doing this properly is to take the time to drive the boat around for a while and explore as much of the water as possible, then sit back and decide what looks best and begin there. Putting together a game plan is really part of the fun in fishing. It is not a wise judgement call to die in one spot all day long knowing that ten years ago a big fish was taken there. Fishing with live bait often means a very slow and cautious saturation of an area, so take the time to select the areas to be fished carefully.

How long should you fish one area before moving? This, of course, is a commonly asked question. There is no exact time frame to work with here. Everything depends on what happens while the lines are out. If absolutely no action takes place in the first spot selected within a half hour, and area has been fished thoroughly, then move to spot number two and repeat the procedure. One point to take note of is being sure the boat and your baits are where they should be. It is easy to drop anchor twenty yards off the drop-off and not know it, or to drift away from the sunken island or point. Keep your casts and baits in the prime waters near the breaks and weed edges to insure the highest odds of finding fish. If pike are in the area, it should take no longer than thirty minutes to get a strike, but make sure different depths and size baits are tried before leaving.

Summer pike in many lakes love feeding in very heavy weeds. These areas are often full of bull rushes, reeds and assorted "junk" weeds of all types. Water clarity will govern how shallow the pike will roam to feed. Some lakes and rivers are very dirty, and pike feed in only two feet of water! While in others where the water is crystal clear, the pike very seldom travel shallower than five feet. The thickness of the actual weed bed often determines if the pike will stay in shallow water or not. The ideal situation for the angler is when the weeds do not choke the surface completely, but a solid foundation of weeds cover the bottom.

Shallow water pike action is best in early morning and evening when the pike are more interested in roaming from the weedy hide-outs. Anglers can do very well if lures are selected to go right into the weedy areas and actually hit the pike on the nose! Topwater baits have their moments here because they can be fished above the weeds, but they are only effective in very clear lakes, or in places where the pike are known to be shallow. Spinnerbaits are the preferred choice for shallow weeds, and bucktails for deeper weeds. Large blades on these lures make a great amount of flash and water resistance as they spin to slow lure speed down, so the big pike can have more time to find it in the jungle of weeds.

Polarized sunglasses make it possible to spot many shallow water places pike may be lurking. The weedline edge is often

Author Tom Zenanko admires a fine pike taken on a muskie "jerk" bait called the Suick. Many of the best muskie tactics also pay off big for anglers looking for large northern pike.

not visible to the naked eye, but with the glare reducing polarized lenses, the weed edges, pockets and drop-offs can be easily seen on most lakes. This tip is mentioned only briefly, but it is one that is **EXTREMELY** important to successful fishing in shallow water.

Anglers are always looking for excuses why they did not catch any pike. One common example occurs during the summer months while the pike are loosing their teeth. Since the pike have sore mouths, they just will not bite! This old wives tale still brings a smile to my face when I here it used. What really happens at this time of year to give anglers the impression that the pike have sore mouths begins with their year-round shedding of teeth. As any pike grows, it's teeth are constantly breaking off and new teeth are growing in to replace them. The warmer water temperatures that come with summer, make it possible for small amounts of infection to swell up the area around the teeth and gums for a short period. This "sore mouth" excuse has been used long enough. Pike continue to feed with or without a sores in the mouth.

The growing and shedding of teeth on a northern pike goes on all year. Only during the warm summer months do anglers visually see the swelling and sores caused as the teeth are lost.The warmer waters permit small areas of infection to swell up before the pike can heal completely. A sore mouth is NOT a reason for poor fishing success.

Fall Pike Tactics

As the days of summer shorten, the beginning of the fall season offers some of the finest pike fishing many anglers will see for big fish all season! The end of August and into early September are the months which start the fall season to the pike, and this means time to start eating! The first growing and feeding peak of the season is in March, but many of the popular pike waters are closed to fishing. This fall feeding frenzy is the second time in a season the big pike simply go crazy.

Many experts have tried to figure out where the big pike suddenly re-appear from. This is one of the great mysteries of pike fishing. The big pike begin to appear in weedbeds and many other shallow water areas that held nothing but small fish all season.

Surface buzzing or skittering is one technique that works well in areas where pike move into deep water weed beds for their fall feeding frenzy. Weeds found rising almost to the surface in six to ten feet of water can qualify as skittering water.

The first skittering or surface buzzing was done some years ago using twenty foot cane poles, twenty-five feet of fifty pound test line and a large spoon. Today the tools of the surface buzzer have changed little, only large plugs are also being used along with the large spoons.

The angler trolls the boat at a fairly quick pace over the largest areas of deep water weed beds in the lake. The long

The long cane poles used in skittering make it possible to quickly lift the lure out of the water when snagged in weeds. Big pike are just not scared off by the motor, which can make for some exciting northern fishing.

cane poles are still commonly used today, and for a very good reason. The extra long shafts aid in the process of lifting the large lures out of the water to remove the weeds which almost constantly hook the lures. Short rods and heavy duty bait casting gear can be used in the same fashion, but it requires more effort to reel in the lures every time a weed clings to it.

The spoons and plugs are right in the prop wash of the motor as an erratic trolling path is made over the weeds. It is hard to believe that a big pike would come up to grab a lure right behind an outboard motor, but they do! This method of fishing the weed flats on a lake during the fall is not a one lake method. It has produced pike and even trophy muskie from waters all across the country.

The way a pike is landed with a cane pole depends on the weight of the fish. Once the very visible strike occurs, the fish is right near the surface and violently tries to get free. The long flexible cane poles bow to the power of the fish. In many cases, the fish is tamed just by raising and lowering the long rod. If the fish is too large to battle, then it is wise to simply release the cane pole and let the pike drag it around for a short distance. Once the pike is given a few minutes to run, pick up the cane pole off the water and continue the battle!

The early fall feeding frenzy is also the time many of the best muskie baits are equally effective for big pike.

Bucktails and jerkbaits of all kinds have a whole new meaning with pike anglers at this time of year. By working over the tops of the large and deep weed flats, big pike can be drawn up to the surface from ten feet of water or more if the lures have enough flash and action to make it worth their while. Over sized spinners and curly tail rubber worms added to the hooks will permit the lures to be fished slowly, but yet shallow enough to run above the weeds without getting tangled in them.

The strike can often be visually seen in many cases with polarized sunglasses.These glare reducing glasses also make it possible to direct casts into pockets or along weed edges to keep the lure in more productive areas. Casting heavy lures all

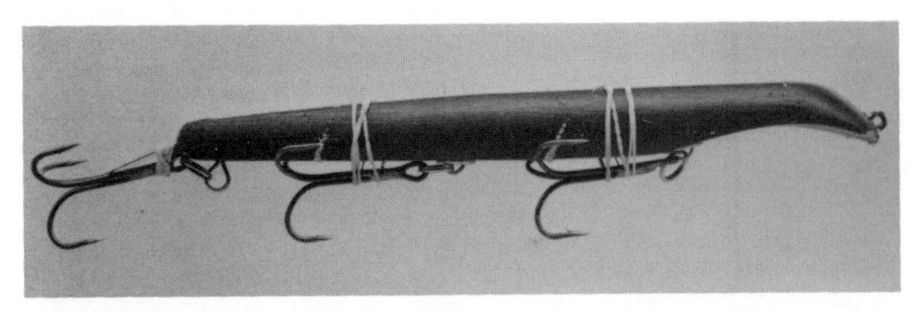

One tip for anglers looking to fish a "jerk" bait or other plug above a thick weedbed is to attach rubber binders around the lure. This makes it possible for the hooks to ride tight to the lure and free of many weeds, but will quickly break away from the lure when a fish strikes.

day, especially ones with large spinners that are difficult to drag through the water, can make fishing seem like hard work, but it does add a new bite of suspense that trolling can never supply.

Bobber rigs are often used at this time of year to suspend large live suckers above the weeds. This is one time of year where it really might pay to use a larger than normal sucker. If the minnow continually pulls the bobber under in attempts to reach the weed beds below, then break off or cut the tail fin of the minnow. This will permit the minnow to swim like crazy, but not go anywhere! A small spinner just above the hook is often a good idea as the roaming pike will be able to key in on the bait with the extra little flash created as the minnow swims about. A good guideline to follow when setting bobber depth in weeds is to set the bait at half the distance to the bottom. In most cases, this will put the sucker or large shiner just above the weed growth and in the path of hungry northern pike.

The big pike will continue to use the thick weed beds until they begin to turn brown and die for the winter. At this point areas which still have green weeds can hold some great fish, but the majority of the pike action will shift out to the major points and areas with lots of sand or rock. The big pike are often still shallow and can be taken in areas abundant with food, and since the dying weedbeds can no longer serve as a home for the baitfish. They move to sandy or rocky areas to feed, and the pike follow right behind!

The colder the weather gets, the more important bait fishing techniques come into play. Even dead bait rigs begin to produce fish now. They seem especially effective when used outside weedy areas that were heavily fished during the major feeding frenzy. Wind blown areas often attract pike to feed on fish who are feeding on the organisms pushed to shore by the waves. Wave action is more critical to fish movements in the fall than at any other time of year. Wind swept rocks or sand points in the fall are simply ideal situations for finding big pike. The colder and more miserable the weather gets, the more pike tend to be active in the fall!

Since the fall turn-over has taken place in most lakes by this time, the water's oxygen levels and temperatures are mixed, so the pike can roam to any depth that feels comfortable. This means a wider variety of depths and locations must be tried to find the areas where the pike are grouped together. Anglers should always relate to the bottom first in the fall, and if that does not work, use a bobber rig to suspend the baits above the bottom moving the baits toward the surface in three feet intervals.

Winter Pike Strategies

The winter pike fishing season begins as the first layers of ice cover the water. This time of the year will involve almost exclusive use of bait fishing techniques. Both live and dead bait methods have proven to be effective during the first portion of this cold weather season, with dead bait methods becoming more and more effective as winter wears on.

The first line of business is to select an area to fish. Here the use of electronic depth finders again can be brought into play. These units will give instant depth readings right through the ice, too! Many of the prime areas to fish early in the winter season will be very close to where fall fishing action was found. Points and outside edges of weed lines still hold many pike for at least the first month after the ice has formed.

Minnesota is one state which permits winter spearing of northern pike. Small windowless shacks are placed in and around the shallow weed edges of a lake and with a large hole chopped in the ice, an imitation minnow or "decoy" is dropped below the hole to catch the attention of a nearby pike. Once the pike swims up to the decoy for a closer look it is killed by a large harpoon. This practice of spearing northern pike is grounds for heavy debate in Minnesota, and it is the sincere hope of every sportfishing organization that this wintertime slaughter of pike be ended.

Much of the early season pike action is done in shallow water, so anglers placing lines must be aware that sounds do travel through the ice and can spook a big pike away. Many of the best pike fishermen believe northern fishing is best before

Ice fishing for northern pike can be challenging and rewarding. These two young anglers had the time of their lives trying to get this beauty out of a small hole.

the ice is thick enough to drive cars, after that point, the big fish are just too spooked in the shallows to be caught while cars and snowmobiles travel above them.

Since shallow water pike are easily spooked under the ice, it often pays to cover the holes with carpet or even a piece of cardboard to prevent the beam of sunlight shining down the hole and alerting the pike.

A good tip to remember when ice fishing after the first snow, is to cover the hole.On open hole permits a bright beam of light to shine down in an area of darkness. The pike may be spooked by the light or just stay away from it.By covering the hole with carpet or cardboard, the pike will not be alarmed.

There are many different ways in which ice fishermen store and handle their fishing lines. The "tip-up" is by far one of the most popular devices to come along in years. They are made in many different shapes and sizes, all claiming that brand X is better than brand Y.

A small spool contains the main line, which is very heavily braided nylon or even a thick level taper fly line. This spool is then suspended under water, since under water, the spool will be permitted to spin freely and not freeze solid between strikes. A small flag or alarm system is triggered if the spool begins spinning to signal a strike.

Anglers not using a tip-up rig, end up rapping line around the outside of the hole so the fish will be permitted to run off at least ten feet before the angler can personally feed out more line. On a cold and windy day, the advantages of a tip-up rig are priceless.

A tip-up is commonly used by winter pike anglers. It is designed so the spool containing your line is submerged under water to prevent freezing. The flag will trigger to alert anglers of a strike as the submerged spool feeds out the needed line.

The standard bobber rigs like those used during the summer months are often used, but it is important in winter fishing that the bait always be parallel to the bottom. This is especially true for dead bait rigs. Start placing the lines three feet above the bottom and keep moving them toward the surface at three foot intervals every half hour if there is no response.

Pike found in fifteen feet of water or less are usually very aggressive as winter pike anglers will hope to get in on some action in shallow water. If no fish have been taken in an hours time, then is is wise to move around a bit. Simply moving to deeper water nearby can often bring results.

Late season pike action will find northerns suspending far above the bottom. It is not unusual to find big pike hanging around schools of crappie. One example of how big pike will suspend with schools of crappie in the winter occurred a few years ago on a lake not far from my home. My father and I were after some fresh crappie for dinner and when we got to the lake, we set up a small portable fish house right near hundreds of other houses and people fishing out in the open. The action was fast, and within an hour we were just a few fish short of our limit. Suddenly my bobber floated to its side and figuring it was a strike, a quick pull produced nothing, as the line was brought up to check the bait, another line was attached to mine. Handing one end to my father we proceeded to pull in this line, suddenly there was a strong pull on my end of the line and at that moment my father pulled in a large sucker still attached to a big hook and leader. Suddenly realizing I had hooked the line of another fisherman, who was only about twenty feet away standing on the ice. Rather than just letting the line go, we decided to act like a big pike! This guy was yelling and screaming with every run we made, and several times we had every inch of line off his spool before giving some slack. While this little joke was going on I could not decide a good way to end the fight. Should I take off the sucker and replace it with a note saying "Sorry Charlie"? At one point my father even went outside to lend any support this fisherman might need. After about fifteen minutes of non-stop laughter, we decided to cut up the minnow with a knife and send it all back down the hole. At least thirty people by now were gathered around the hole, but all hopes vanished as the shredded minnow came up through his hole.

This missed fish sent shock waves all across the lake and before long everybody began fishing with big sucker minnows trying to catch the big one that got away. Not realizing that big pike often follow schools of crappie around, I was simply shocked as nearby anglers started pulling in pike one right after another up to sixteen pounds! The guy who missed the biggest fish in the lake ended up with a limit that averaged over ten pounds!

From that point on, whenever large schools of crappie or even sunfish are found, at least one line was rigged for pike fishing. It is wise to run this line at or slightly below the depth the crappie are being caught at for best success.

The strike when ice fishing for pike seems to be more violent than when summer fishing, but this can be misleading. Movement in any direction ends up pulling the bobber under the ice. Do not be fooled into thinking that just because the bobber is under a foot of ice, the pike has still got the bait in his mouth. The first run of the pike is often the most violent, but there never seems to be two northern that act the same. Wait until the fish has begun to move off for a second time before striking. When multiple hook rigs are used, anglers are often free to set the hooks at the first sign of a strike to avoid gut hooking pike. Any damage to the gills or internal organs of the northern as a result of being deeply hooked often results in slow death for the pike.

Northern pike action during the middle of the day during winter is quite common. As winter wears on, pike action seems to peak later and later into the afternoon. There is also a noticeable movement of the pike toward the deepest portions of the lake. The pike do not necessarily need to hug the bottom either. As water temperatures continue to cool, pike often suspend high above the bottom. This makes for a very challenging task of finding a preferred depth to suspend baits at, but with a little trial and error it often does not take long to find them.

The true intrigue in catching a big pike through a small hole in the ice makes for a real challenge that will test the skills of any angler. Granted there is not really much to do when you are staring down a hole watching the ice slowly begin to recover the hole, but the blood really starts to pump when a firm hookset is made by hand and the power of the struggling pike sends line screaming through your fingers.

The procedure for hooking and landing a pike begins with one word, **PREPARATION!** There are many things which must be done to prepare the line for a one-on-one battle. First, enough extra line must be out on the ice and free from tangles so if the pike does make a big run, line is ready to freely unwind. Even after the hookset is made, the line must be coiled in some kind of organized pile once more, if the fish does make a run, there will be plenty of free line available. Fighting the fish is done with a hand over hand motion and doing this without gloves is preferred. Squeeze the line between the thumb and forefinger with equal pressure each time the line is grabbed,

Ice fishing for northern pike is one of the best seasons to catch a large pike, but even a small fish can bring a warm smile to a young angler.

as there will never be a time when slack or too much tension is put on the fish. A good pike will make several runs under the ice before its nose begins to bump the ice. This is a sign that the battle is nearing an end. Do not think that the pike is down and out yet, being able to make one last run seems to be their trademark, and the unprepared angler is left with a broken line.

Getting a pike through a small hole in the ice is sometimes done by hand or with a short gaff. The holes for pike fishing should be no less than eight inches across. All sharp or rough edges of the hole should be chipped away to eliminate any chance of the line being snagged while the pike is darting around under the ice.

Obviously small pike can be lifted right out of the hole without too much of a hassle, but pike four pounds or more begin to require a little more finesse in getting the fish pointed up the hole properly. The real trick in getting a pike to swim right up your hole is to understand that fish cannot swim backwards! Once the nose of the pike is pointed up the hole, it is very easy to guide the fish up to the surface with a steady pressure on the line. It is critical to remember that while in the water a twenty pound fish is weightless, but as soon as its nose hits the air, the true weight of the pike can put excess stress on the hook or line and the fish could simply fall back down the hole.

Getting a big fish out of a hole should be done with a small gaff hook. This is by far the safest and most reliable method of getting a pike out of the hole. With one continuous motion, the hook of the gaff must be secured into the bottom of the pike's jaw, which is the softest part of the body in the hole. The biggest problem with a gaff is that unless the pike is pulled out of the hole quick enough, they can very easily flop off the gaff and slip back into the hole.

Grabbing a pike by hand is risky business and is not recommended. Too many times pike teeth or fish hooks cut the fingers or arm of an excited angler. Only when there is no other way to get a large fish out of the hole should landing a pike with unprotected hands be used. The procedure begins by making extra sure the pike has been played out. Once the nose of the pike is on the surface, the angler must reach down along the back of the fish and pinch inward very hard behind the gill plates. This must be done with only one hand, while the other keeps a steady pressure on the line so the pike doesn't slip back down the hole. When grabbing the fish by gaff or hand, it is important to make the move to get the pike out of the hole as quickly as possible, without putting any extra pressure on the hook or line.

The eye socket method of lifting a big pike out of a hole is extremely difficult and risky, this method of holding or carrying pike is one which is best forgotten about for nearly all applications of pike fishing. There will be much more said about this way of handling pike later.

CHAPTER EIGHT

Care and Handling of Pike

Since the beginning of time, humans have relied on fish as a major source of food. Catching fish for survival is something which has faded away with our modern-day living habits, but still there is the desire to keep at least some fish for food.

In the last ten years, anglers across the country have started to change their tune of catching fish just for food. Sportsman's groups began appearing as people started to realize the use of fishing as a sport. Fishing in some regions of northern Canada had already been abused, true sportsmen began educating fishermen on the importance of "catch and release" fishing. The fish and game departments in many states have begun extensive stocking programs to increase the sportfishing opportunities in their areas. This has been one of the major reasons for the northern pike's increasing range.

A whole new age of respect for the sport of fishing is on the horizon. More and more fishermen are now heading out on the water fishing for fun and not to fill the freezer. Fishing offers a great release from the frustrations of modern day living, and people from all walks of life are discovering its true pleasures. The pike is actually one of last gamefish to be accepted by fishermen as a fish worth catching. This book, along with magazine stories and many of the conservation groups are hoping more anglers realize the pike is an outstanding sportfish.

"Catch and release" fishing is gaining popularity all over the world, simply because fishermen are realizing the future of fishing rests on letting the fish go to fight again another day. Learning the proper techniques of playing, netting and releasing pike is very important.

One of the disadvantages of fishing for pike with light tackle is the fish are often played out for too long a time, and the pike becomes overly exhausted. When this happens there is a very dangerous build up of lactic acid in the blood which chokes off the supply of oxygen to the pike and causes death. One of the visual signs of this happening is blood dripping from the tail fins or sides of the pike.

Another factor which can cause death is how the pike is handled once it is out of the water. In the weightless environ-

It is wise to use the proper tools to remove the hooks from any size pike. Fishermen must always respect the unpredictable pike whenever they are to be handled.

ment of water, the pike's bone structure and internal organs have no pressure on them in any way. Once the pike is lifted out of the water, extreme stress is put on the body of the pike. It is difficult to know what kind of internal damage has been done to a fish that slowly swims away after being caught.

"Playing out" a big pike can be done in a wide variety of ways. Some anglers using heavy tackle and strong line to simply reel-in a pike giving it hardly a chance to fight. On the other hand, some may prefer long light action rods for pike fishing that may take up to a thirty minutes to land one fish! For the sake of releasing the fish, the faster the northern is landed and released, the better the odds are the pike will recover properly to strike again someday.

Successfully landing a big pike is something which will test your equipment and rigs their fullest, and being prepared is the real secret to not missing a trophy once it is hooked.

The reel's drag system should be pre-set to eliminate any last

"The proper pose" when working an artificial lure, keep the rod tip down. As a northern pike strikes, it is now possible to quickly raise the rod tip and firmly set the hooks.

minute confusion. This is done by simply pulling on the line to estimate the pounds of pressure needed to make the drag slip. A good rule to follow is to set the drag at is one quarter the total strength of the line. Skilled anglers will set the drag much heavier to insure better hooksets and fish control in heavy vegetation. This use of a tight drag is not recommended with light lines, or using fishing lures with small hooks, as both could easily give way with one powerful run.

When the time comes to set the hooks on a big pike, there is only one phrase to stress the importance of how hard the hooks must be set, **"RIP THOSE LIPS!"** The boney jaw of the pike makes it almost impossible for a hook to penetrate unless a strong hookset is made. A rod with a "soft action" can make setting the hook hard difficult if not impossible. For anglers preferring the use of lighter tackle, there is one trick in hooksetting that is worth a try. The pike have a soft spot located on each corner of the jaw. The Europeans call this spot the "scissors" as it joins together the upper and lower jaws. When the time comes to strike a pike with light tackle, be sure the fish has had time to turn and swim away before any extra pres-

The "scissors" of the pike is one toothless area in the mouth where anglers using light tackle can get a hook to hold.Lucky anglers fishing without leaders often find they have accidentally hooked a northern pike in the "scissors" otherwise the sharp teeth would have quickly cut the line.

sure is put on the fish. This hooksetting method can be tricky when artificial lures are used. The pike should be given a fraction of a second to turn away before the hookset, the chances of the hook slipping into the "scissors" is very good.

During the actual battle, a large pike is capable of coiling its body into an "S" shape, by quickly straightening the body, the pike zips forward. This unique style of battle is the reason pike have such a great reputation for breaking lines and why three pound fish can seem comparable to a ten or fifteen pounder. Actual pike swimming speeds range from only three to eight miles per hour. It is the northern's sudden burst of speed which causes so many broken lines.

Even when a pike seems beaten, there always seems to be one more run. Anglers should keep that rod tip high during the battle to anticipate any of their line breaking tricks.

Rod control along with a good drag system can bring in any size pike. By keeping the rod tip high in the air while the pike is hooked, will make it possible to drop the rod tip to follow the fish as it runs. The reason the rod must be kept high is to avoid any sudden shock to the line and makes it possible for the reel's drag to take over from this point on. On some occasions the entire rod may be submerged to follow the power of a hard fighting male pike.

The sure sign that a pike is done fighting is when its nose can be held slightly above the water. This is one tip light tackle anglers should make special note of. By keeping the nose of the pike out of the water, it is impossible for the pike to catch their breath. Water can not flow through the mouth and over the gills, which makes it hard for the pike to breath. Even though the pike appears to be beat, do not think for a second that there is not one last jump or head shake left. Now would be the best time to get the net prepared.

Landing nets are like an insurance policy, nobody likes to carry them around, but they seem priceless when you need them. The bigger the net, the easier it is to land a large pike. In most boats, a big net just seems to get in the way too much. a good substitute for a large net would be to carry a smaller net, but make sure it has a deep mesh bag to handle a long fish.

The mesh bags can be the cause of many missed fish unless the angler takes the time and a few dollars to replace the netting after a few years. A quick visual inspection will show if the netting is frayed or rotting.

The longer handled nets make it easier to land a long fish, but at the same time, stay away from nets that have a piece of plastic joining the hoop to the handle. This plastic link breaks under the pressure of a big fish in the net. Whenever possible, select nets with metal connecting sleeves.

Netting a Pike

It was a beautiful summer day several years ago when my parents went on a fishing trip with Uncle John. The scene has happened many times with anglers all over the world, but is relived at every family gathering.

My uncle was the real fishermen of the group because he owned an outboard motor and a tackle box full of secret lures. My father was proud to be fishing with his new fishing outfit that his girl friend (my mother) had given him for his birthday. It was the newest solid steel rod on the market equipped with fifty pound braided silk line.

This kind of fancy gear was new to my father and he didn't have any lures to use with it, because he was really more a panfish angler. A polite request was made to borrow a lure of any type from the large chest size tackle box owned by my uncle.

"I had no intention of giving him anything I thought would catch a fish because he had a nicer rod and reel outfit I did," remembered my uncle. Reaching to the bottom of the box, he pulled out a jointed plug that was a foot long and looked as if it was made from a broom stick.

"Here, this is one of my best baits, and if you lose it, I'll charge you ten bucks!" warned my sly uncle. Father humbly agreed and attached the large plug to his heavy line. Everyone was waiting to see the first big cast with the new outfit. The old style bait casting reels in those days demanded a great deal of practice to avoid backlashes. Since dad had never fished with such a fancy outfit, the first cast ended with a large backlash. A chuckle came from my uncle's boat as he now started up his motor to headed to one of his favorite spots.

By this time dad had taken the "bird's nest" out of the reel and began to retrieve the line lying all over the seat. "I'm snagged now, too," commented my father, who was beginning to turn a little red by this time. With a quick glance, Uncle John knew there was a fish on his line because he realized there were no weeds on that end of the lake and that the old plug he had given my father was a floating plug.

Meanwhile, dad had no idea what was happening as the large clump of "weeds," came slowly towards the boat. Suddenly the huge pike came into view with the lure laying crosswise in his mouth like a dog with a bone.The lazy female just loomed on the surface and stared at the boat. No fight, it just floated under the surface lake a big alligator.

"Grab her!" shouted my father to my speechless mother as the two just sat there staring at this huge northern pike that was staring right back at them. Suddenly my mother shouts, "it's too big!!!" Struggling to operate the new fishing outfit, my father looked at my mother and demanded she reach down and grab the pike and lift it into the boat. At that moment the northern decided to make a run for it, and with a flip of her enormous tail, under the boat she swam.

By this time, dear old uncle was yelling directions to my father and was also trying to get close enough to throw them a landing net. Seeing the tail fin of the pike surface above water, my uncle knew a thirty pound pike was on the line and there was no time to waste. Unfortunately, the new reel had a direct drive feature, as dad was having a tug-of-war contest with thirty pounds of northern pike. Within a few seconds, the line was broken and the shock of what had just happened was setting in. My father ended the day right there and refused to talk to his girl friend (my future mother) for nearly two weeks!

When a pike is on the surface and ready to be netted, be sure to scoop it HEAD first into the net for best results.

The procedure for netting a big pike is simple, and takes a short period of time to master. Netting begins as soon as the pike's nose is on the surface. This is when the net should be taken out of its holding place and organized. Too many times the net is one of the first things excited anglers start digging for when a fish is hooked and too much effort is put into untangling the net rather than fighting the fish. This is why it is nice if more than one angler is in the boat, because one can enjoy fighting the pike while the other gets the net ready. Being distracted with a tangled net is the last thing that should be on your mind as a pike makes a powerful run under the boat. Take one thing at a time and fight the fish first.

DO NOT put the landing net in the water before the fish is actually netted. Instead, keep the net in the boat, free from oar locks and fishing reels which could snag the netting. Remembering that fish do not swim backwards, the goal will be to

Experience is one of the best teachers of all. When a big fish is ready to be lifted into the net, grab the hoop. Net with plastic sleeves to join the hoop and the handle often can not take the strain of a big fish.

"skim" the pike off the surface **HEAD FIRST.** If at any point the fish is under the water more than a few inches, **DO NOT** try to net it! One complete pass with the net must be able to reach both the head and tail of the fish in one non-stop motion. A commonly made mistake is to reach out with the net and try to tuck in a long fish that is too far from the boat. By the time half of the fish is in, the other half is out and flops back out of the net. Scooping the fish head first with a fast and steady motion until the tail is in the net is important.

When the northern is in the net, the tricky part is to quickly lift the net and swing it into the boat. The problem of netting a big northern pike is that the hoop often cannot take the pressure, and breaks at the sleeve where the hoop meets the handle. Even if the net has a metal sleeve connecting the hoop and handle, the net could still break. The best way to lift a big pike out of the water is by grabbing the hoop. This will insure the pike will not flop out of the net or break the handle.

While in the boat, a northern pike is a very dangerous animal looking for a chance to stick a hook into an arm or leg. If the pike is one you plan to keep, it is best to club and kill the pike before any hooks are removed. Extreme caution can never be stressed enough when handling a newly caught pike.

If the northern is to be released, it is wise to have the proper tools ready for quick and easy hook removal. Many anglers question even using nets to bring a fish out of the water at all if it is to be released. The more the fish is handled, the greater the chances are of the fish dying. Only anglers with a great amount of experience in handling live pike should attempt this kind of release technique. By netting the fish first, it will be much safer and if done quick enough, not too harmful to the pike.

Four tools should be kept in the pike anglers boat at all times. A mouth spreader used to force the mouth of the pike open; A long nose hook remover, for reaching deep down into the mouth of the pike; A pair of long nose pliers; and a pair of wire cutters which must be strong enough to cut the largest hook in the

Once that trophy pike is in the net, be sure to reach up and bring the fish into the boat by grabbing the hoop. Most nets will break right where the handle and hoop meet, so don't take any chances, grab the hoop!

tackle box. These four tools are priceless in helping reduce a pike's time spent out of water. Wire cutters are handy if an angler has been hooked by the pike. Cutting the hook is the quickest and easiest way of removing a badly embedded hook if the fish is still attached to the lure.

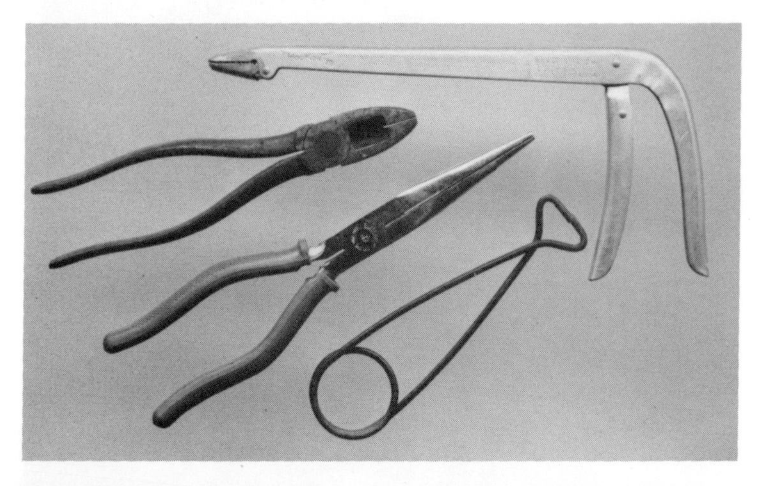

Having the right tools along on every trip is a wise idea. They are a very cheap form of insurance when handling or unhooking a pike.

The pike at no time should be held by the eye sockets! For years anglers were wrong in thinking that pinching the eye sockets of a pike was the best way to control them. The eyes are very fragile in a pike and if damaged in any way, blindness will result.

Grabbing the pike across the back and squeezing just behind the gill covers is one secure way of lifting pike. Another would be inserting one or two fingers under the gill plate without

DO NOT handle a pike to be released in this manner because blindness will result or lead to a slow death for released pike.

damaging the gills. Many pike anglers prefer to carry cotton gloves in the boat to protect their hands when handling pike. Gloves can give the angler a better hold on the slippery pike. At the same time, the gloves tend to remove the valuable slim coating on the fish which protects it from disease and infection. It is a good idea to have a old pair of gloves in the boat as the gills and teeth of a pike can really cause some painful cuts.

Once the hooks have been removed, the pike should be quickly placed back in the water. **DO NOT THROW** the pike into the water, especially a big pike, because it will need time to recover from the shock of being caught. With a few short minutes of

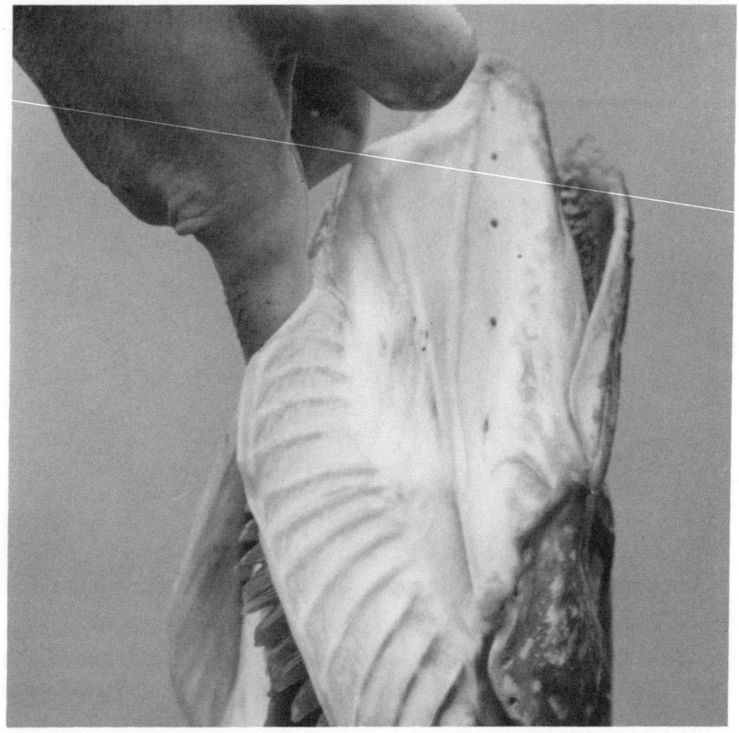

The top photo shows where to grasp a pike for easy and safe handling when removing hooks. The bottom photo shows where the fingers can be inserted under the gill plate to lift a larger pike. It is critical with this method not to damage the gills in any way.

care, the pike will quickly recover and be able to swim away under its own power. This is done by holding the tail section of the pike while it is in the water and slowly moving the fish back and forth. The time it will take for each fish to recover will vary greatly. Water temperature, time out of the water and how long the fish was fought all play a part in deciding recovery time. Any pike taking over five minutes to recover will have a very slim chance of surviving.

Once the strength of the pike has come back and the fish seems back to normal, release it in water no deeper than ten feet. This will insure the pike will be in water rich in oxygen and the constant water temperatures in shallow water will aid the pike's recovery time.

This twenty pound pike would have died if the angler did not take the time to work the fish back and forth in the water while holding onto the tail.This simple release procedure can save many pike during the course of a season.

Keeping your Catch

The eating quality of the northern pike is loved by millions and rightly so, the light flaky meat has only one percent fat, which makes it one fish people can eat day after day. As long as the pike are going to be put to good use, and not being used to fill every freezer in the neighborhood, the killing of a few pike for personal consumption is a great idea.

One of the major risks with any fish is the rapid rate in which the meat deteriorates once the fish dies. The proper care of the fish, especially northern pike with their flaky white meat is essential. Far too many great eating pike are wasted when anglers get lazy or forgetful.

Fish stringers are commonly used to hold pike in the water while fishing. The wire chain type stringers should never be used, in fact any of the clip type stringers will prove to be very weak and should be avoided if possible. Only heavy-duty rope stringers are recommended. Stringers can be used to hold pike at any time of year, but a good size pike in mid-summer when the water is warm, runs a good chance of dying because they use up too much strength to fight and can not recover. Ideally, a fish stringer will work best during the cool spring months and again in the fall.

To attach a rope stringer, the angler must be sure to thread the rope through **BOTH** lips of the pike. This will insure that while moving the pike from one area to another when trolling, the act of forcing the water into the mouth will not cause the fish to drown. This can easily happen if the stringer is threaded through only one lip of the fish. **NEVER** thread the rope through the gills of a pike at any time. Pike need gills to breath and any damage to them will mean death!

When stringers are used for holding pike, be sure to check the pike while fishing to see if enough stringer line has been given so the pike's head is under water. Too many times a fish is quickly attached and thrown over the side with barely its tail touching the water! Watching for the motor is another common mistake when a fish is placed over the side. The long bodies of the pike often extend much further back toward the motor than originally planned and the pike get chopped up.

A live well is one option for holding pike without the use of stringers. A large watertight container is installed in a boat and filled with water. A water pump furnishes fresh water to the fish in the tank as if they were in an aquarium. Live wells do a fine job of holding smaller pike, but most tanks are not large enough to hold a big northern.

Many anglers use the traditional wet burlap sack for keeping the pike fresh. The cooling action created as the wet burlap tries to dry iteslf does an outstanding job of keeping the pike from spoiling. When a fish dies and is left to soak up water, when put on a stringer or placed in a live well, pike flesh begins to absorb water which can make for some terrible tasting fillets. Much of the confusion made when anglers take fish from a lake which taste weedy, oily or are just plain mushy is often due to improper care of the fish after it has been caught. The burlap sack trick prevents the fish from spoiling and protects any foul odors from contaminating the meat.

Another simple way of insuring better tasting pike is to place them on ice as soon as they have been caught. This, of course, is hard to do if a large pike is caught, but it is the best way of keeping fish fresh before they are cleaned.

One way of knowing if a pike is still eatable is to look at the gills. If they appear white, then there is a very good chance the fish has already spoiled and could taste bad. If the gills are reddish in color, it is a good bet the fish itself is in excellent condition to be eaten.

Another one of those wives tails, concerns the slime of the pike getting on your hands or lures. Many believe that other fish will never touch that lure again if the bitter smelling slime of the northern pike is on the lure. There is no disputing that the sharp smell of northern pike slime is like no other fish, but the affect it has on turning other fish away has never been proven.

CHAPTER NINE

Fishing Electronics

In the last twenty years, fishing has come a long way. One area where great strides have been made is in the field of electronics used for fishing. The use of the first "sonar" units had war-time applications. Today thousands of portable "sonar" units are in use by anglers to find the bottom depths of their favorite lakes. These electronic gadgets are called many different names by anglers all across the country. Fish Finders, Flashers, Sonar, Fish Lo-K-Tors, and Depth Finders all are names for the same style of depth finding device. There are many popular names in the field of fishing electronics, Lowrance, Hummingbird, Si-tex or Vexilar being common names among fishermen across the country. Currently fishermen have several different ways to electronically scan the depth of water under your boat within a fraction of a second. Many of the better units can give excellent depth readings at speeds over 50 miles per hour! It is difficult to look back twenty years when fishermen used a heavy sinker at the end of a line to find a drop-off. Submerged islands were considered truly virgin waters that only the "old timers" knew about. Today if you were to just spend a few minutes zipping around the lake with one of the new high speed depth finding units, it wouldn't take long to learn more about lake than many of the local fishermen who might have fished the lake all their lives! Electronic depth sounding devices can be a big help in catching more fish as long as you can take the time to learn all the interesting facts these gadgets can give you. The Lowrance "green box" was one of the first sonar units adapted for use by the average person. Many of the features found in the first green box are still found in many of the sonar units today. The use of a small rotating and flashing bulb was then, and still is today, the best way of understanding the bottom signals. This spinning bulb displays electronic impulses that are transmitted through a heavy wire called a coax cable to a hockey-puck shaped device called

The traditional "green box" from Lowrance Electronics is one of the most reliable portable sonar units on the market today. Although it has been available for over twenty years now, very little has changed this unit which has become the standard in the industry.

a transducer. This transducer acts like a microphone and speaker all in one to both send and receive electronic impulses generated by the main unit. Looking at the calibrated face of the main unit, a spinning light appears once on the zero mark of the dial and again at the depth of water under the transducer at that exact moment. The depths displayed on the dial are a direct result of the time it takes the signal to reach the bottom and bounce back up to the transducer. This can only take place as long as the transducer is submerged in the water or is in direct contact with it. It is also possible to use these depth finding devices in the winter months. By placing the transducer directly on the ice, the signal will often shoot right through without chopping a hole! If the ice has some bumps of air pockets, it might be difficult to get a good reading. It often pays to use some kind of liquid on the ice to help eliminate any air gaps which can cut off the signal completely. Lake water can be used, but in extremely cold temperatures, water will freeze on the transducer, making it difficult to receive bottom signals.

Looking for an area of clear, dark ice, sonar units of all types are capable of sending a signal right through the ice. Note the bottle of alcohol used to insure an air tight seal between the ice and transducer. Any kind of air pocket can be reason enough for the bottom signal to be lost.

Transducers come in many different shapes which permit them to send and receive a signal while traveling at great speeds through the water. It is **EXTREMELY** important that the transducer be in direct contact with the water to receive a good signal. When the transducer is mounted properly, no matter how fast the boat is traveling, a strong signal should be received.

The type of signal emitted by the transducers will vary because manufacturers give consumers the choice of selecting a very narrow signal of 9 degrees, which can give a very exact depth reading, or a very wide signal of 50 degrees, which scans

By mounting your sonar units in a comfortable position, fishermen will be better able to control the boat. The key here is to sit in the boat the way you feel the most comfortable and then mount the units.

a larger area of the bottom. Although the signal will not be as exact for giving you the depth, with a bit of practice, the signals can be interpreted to tell when a drop-off is nearby or in some cases, even suspended fish. If the consumer is ever given a choice on which type of transducer to select, the models with the widest cone angles should be selected. In the long run, transducers with a wide signal angle will prove to be much more informative.

These depth finding units with rotating bulbs are without a doubt the most practical and effective tool for the northern pike angler. They are simple to operate and in only a few minutes even an amateur will be able to read the basic functions of finding the bottom depth. The on/off switch of the unit is also called the "gain" switch. This gain switch acts like a volume control switch. Turning up the gain all the way, the signal is very strong. By doing this, many of the smaller features in the signal like fish or weeds will be received on the spinning dial.

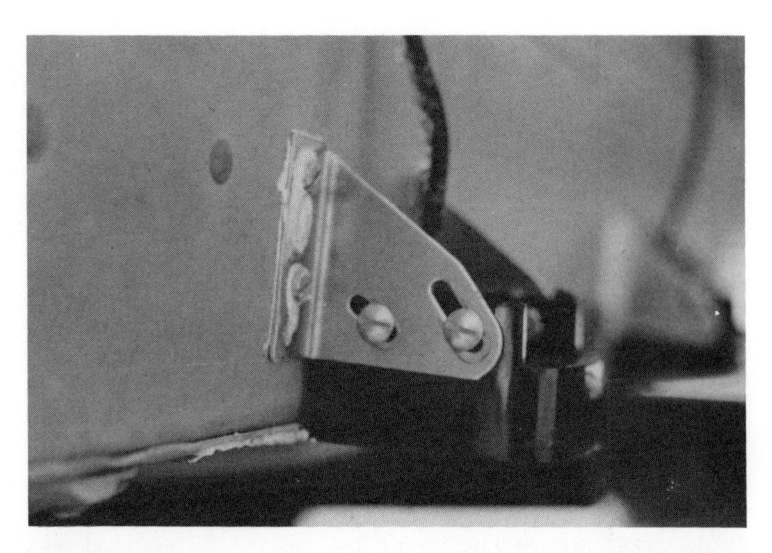

With aluminum boats, the transducers should be mounted outside the boat near the drain plug in the transom.To get a good signal at any speed, be sure to mount the transducer flush with the hull and between any ribs on the hull.A sign that your transducer is mounted too far below the hull is a large rooster tail that shoots up when moving at high speed. If it is not down far enough, the signal will be lost as the boat picks up speed. Minor adjustments in mounting a transducer will always be necessary at first.

Obviously, if the lights start flashing all over the dial and not even the bottom reading can be found, then turn the gain switch down until the bottom signal is easily found. Some of the more refined units have a special knob for noise suppression to keep out interference from motors or other electronic equipment. These suppression knobs should be kept as low as possible, because they will also suppress part of the main signal you will wish to keep very sensitive.

For the cost of $180, it is possible to purchase an excellent flasher unit with a range of 0 to 60 feet, which is all the unit a pike fisherman will ever need. Of course, man's ingenuity has led to many extra features such as night lights, built-in temperature probes, sun visors, swivel mounts, waterproof cases, fish and depth hazard alarms, dual depth scales and the option of having either a portable unit to move from boat to boat, or a

In fiberglass boats, transducers can be mounted inside the boat. This is done by applying silicone or epoxy on a clean surface and the transducer is then put in direct contact with the hull. The drain plug area on most fiberglass boats is the only area where direct contact can be made with the outer hull because most boats have a false bottom. The same can be done with aluminum boats, but expect 30 to 50% reduction in the sensitivity of the unit.

permanently mounted unit. Every season manufacturers are striving to add more innovations to make the flasher type depth finders more appealing.

The depth of water you are in can also be shown by a straight line of LED lights or even a digital read out. The problem with this type of depth finder in comparison to a flasher is their inability to give the extra information a fisherman needs to know about things like bottom make-up, weeds, and fish. This can be helpful at times for putting together the big puzzle of catching more and bigger pike.

Most manufacturers take great time and effort to design an instruction book with the procedures on how to operate each unit. Too many anglers throw these books away and end up in a daze about what knobs to use. It pays to take the time to study any information supplied with the unit to understand all of the features it may have.

Graph Recorders

The most recent breakthrough in fishing electronics is a depth finding unit called a "graph" or "chart recorder." These units work on the same basic principle as the flasher units for sending and receiving bottom signals. The main difference is that the flashes of light seen with a flasher type unit are converted into a surge of electricity to burn the signal into a piece of heat sensitive paper. This type of permanent record of bottom contours adds a new prospective on what the lake looks like, but also a better understanding of the signals received. Graphs have more total output power than a flasher does, so they can tell some interesting facts about the bottom and the fish below that the weaker signals in the flasher could not show. One large fish under the boat with a flasher unit might appear for a fraction

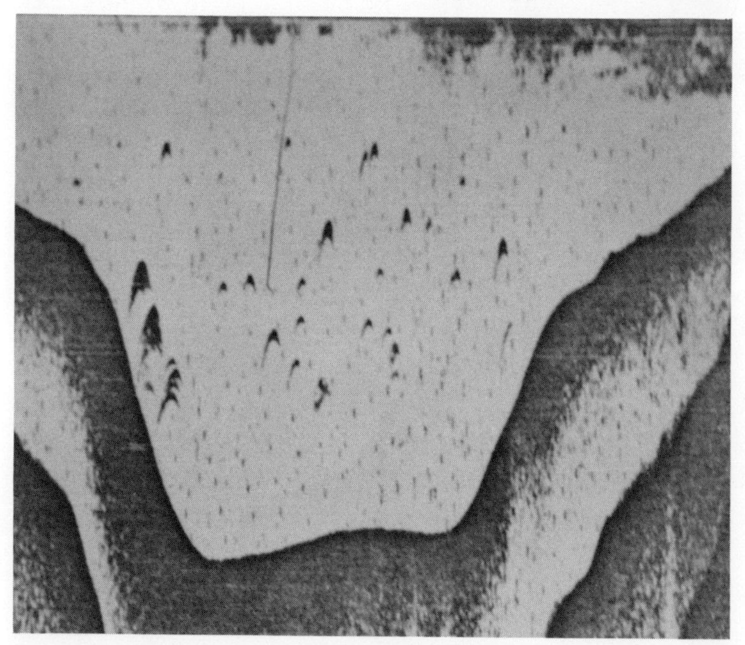

This print out from a graph unit gives a permanent record of how the lake is shaped.The hooked figures drawn here could be trophy pike, or just carp. Knowing something is down there is a real advantage to these types of sonar units, but making them bite is a whole new ballgame.

of a second as a flash just above the bottom. With a graph unit, the fish is permanently marked so the angler knows a fish was below.

The introduction of computer chips in the production of graph recorders has done wonders to bring the computer into thousands of boats. The popular X15 graph made by the Lowrance company was one of the first to make use of computer components to make a small compact graph unit do more things for $500 than most commercial units costing over $2,000! With these new graph units, it is possible to zoom in on the bottom or any depth and take a closer look at signals that may be found there. Any unit on the market today that does not take advantage of the newest computer technology is really out dated!

The newest method of recording bottom signals is with the use of liquid crystals. Very similar to those in watches, these crystals do a fine job of showing the bottom contours, but lack the sharpness that the paper graphs offer. The liquid crystal units have no moving parts to break. A paper graph uses a fine piece of wire on a rotating belt to burn the signal on a special paper.

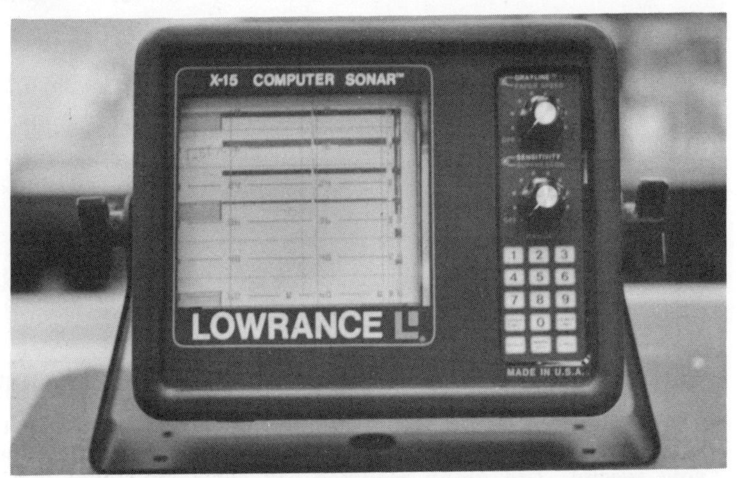

The X-15 graph unit shown here was one of the first to use small computer components to aid the angler with state of the art sonar readings.

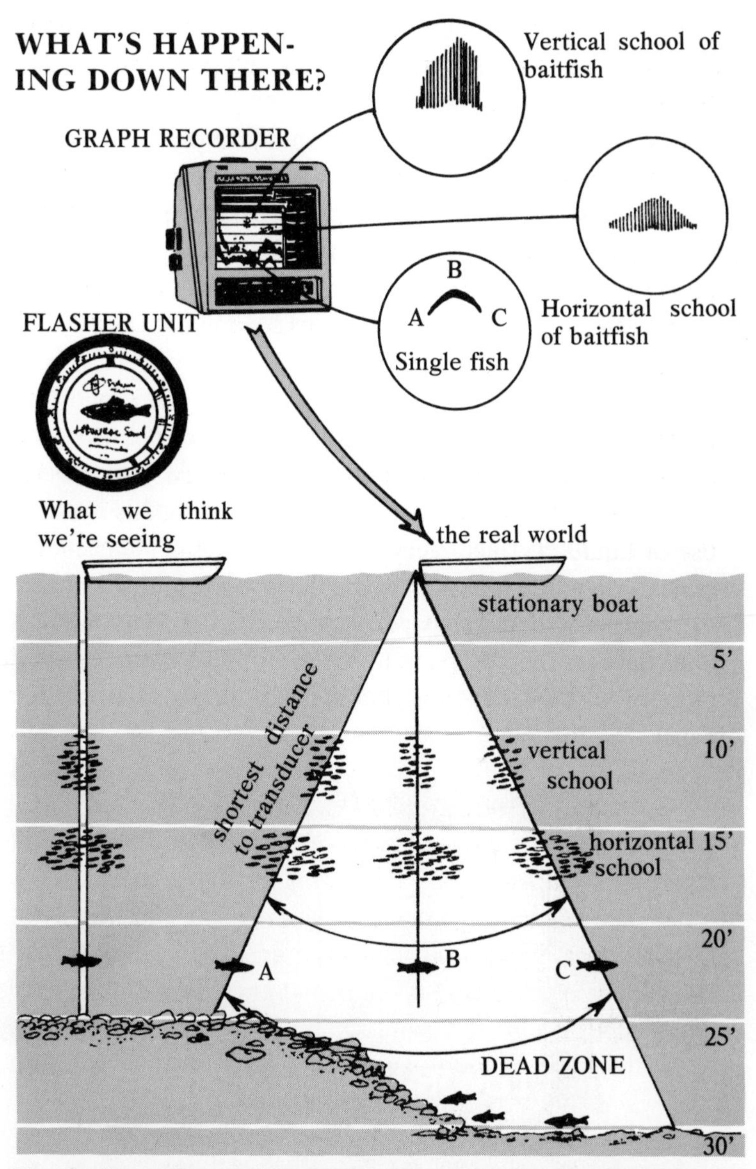

The flasher unit on the left gives you the same readings as the chart unit on the right, but in only a one dimensional view for a split second. The graph readings can show individual fish as hooks. They take this shape as the fish come closer to a direct position under the boat and then leave. Note the dead zone in the signal area created by the small ridge along the bottom. This problem is one of the reasons you can catch fish from an area where the graph shows none!

The avid angler knows no bounds when it comes to new toys and the cost of a good graph-type unit will run $450 to $800. Many of the mounting instructions for graphs are the same for the flashers, but 90% of the graphs are designed to be permanently mounted into the boat. The biggest reason is a graph unit will need a much larger amount of power to run in contrast with a flasher which can be used for a long period of time on two six volt lantern batteries. A twelve volt wet cell battery is the best source of power for any chart recorder to insure good strong signals.

When selecting either a graph or a flasher, the cost of the unit often effects the units overall performance. It is very difficult to recommend one brand over another. As many of the major brands are all striving to out produce each other, the consumer is the one who benefits! Any consumer today should look around and compare prices and warranties. No unit will be trouble free, so **EXPECT** problems, no matter how much you pay. The best priced unit may also turn out to be a unit which takes eight weeks to repair when broke, and not too many fishermen can afford to have their units in a shop for two months of the year. Take note of warranties and locations of service centers to insure good service when it is needed.

The time has come to stress the importance of realizing that even though you own a large assortment of expensive toys is no guarantee of catching huge northern pike. Just like many of the other fancy things that can be purchased in fishing like boron rods or ten thousand dollar boats. There is nothing wrong about owning a ten thousand dollar boat or fifteen rods, because this type of thing can greatly increase your pleasure on the water, but 90% of the time will not directly effect the total weight on the stringer. It is very important to put fishing gadgets into proper perspective. No matter how impressive the sales pitches are and how sophisticated the gadget may be, **YOU** and **YOU** alone are the person who will still be left to hook and fight a big pike!

Knowing where to draw the line on fishing electronics can

be a problem, especially if you subscribe to any number of fishing magazines that are saturated with the advertisements from companies all wanting to out sell each other. The single most important piece of fishing electronics which every fisherman should own would be one of the flasher type depth finding units we have already discussed. Stay away from graphs as long as possible. A flasher unit can give nearly 95% of the bottom information a fisherman would ever need to know at a fraction of the cost compared to a graph unit.

Looking back on history, the unfair advantage of a graph unit as far as what it really can do to your success, dates back to the mid 70's. A bill was introduced in the Minnesota legislature to ban the use of graph recorders. The author of the bill believed that a picture of the bottom and, of course, the fish along the bottom would be an unfair advantage in catching all the fish from a lake, and certainly would ruin the fishing in the entire state! The manufacturers had done such a great job of **OVER** selling the public that everyone began believing these powerful sonar units would be the answer to all the fishless days fishermen have had since the beginning of time! A special study was undertaken at the time by the DNR (Department of Natural Resources) in Minnesota to find out the true effects these units could have on fishing success. Veteran anglers consulted in their reports all concluded that using the graph units did not help catch more fish, **PLAIN** and **SIMPLE.** The bill thereafter had no chance of passing!

Pike Fishing Boats

The nice thing about northern pike is that anglers can get into some great fishing without investing a ton of money, but at the same time anglers want to use only the best and most modern equipment money can buy. The boating industry has come a long way since the birch bark canoe. Like many of the other gadgets in the fishing world, the boats of today are designed to give the greatest amount of fishing pleasure to fishermen.

No matter how hard a boat manufacturer tries to develop a "perfect" fishing boat, it is an impossible task. There are some fantastic fishing boats on the market, but the fisherman today is more prone to use a wider variety of fishing methods compared to their forefathers. This need for more diversified fishing methods makes it very difficult to select one style or type of boat over another. On large lakes, anglers prefer big boats, on small lakes, smaller boats. Some like to look fancy and go fast, while others prefer the slower, less impressive look.

Pike fishing boats can come in all different shapes and sizes. There is really no limit to how much money can be spent on a fishing boat.Take the time to consider what is really needed and select a boat to meet as many of those needs as possible.

It is important when selecting a boat to consider the types of fishing you will hope to do. Anglers fishing on large lakes are advised to think safety first, no fish is ever worth risking your life for. Boat control is the second most important think to consider. Can the motor troll down without fouling spark plugs or is it too heavy for the size of electric motor you currently own? One good way of evaluating your current boat's ability to maneuver at slow speeds is noting how difficult it is to bring the boat along side a dock or another boat. If too much time is spent trying to maneuver it in the right spot, it could mean some big problems of boat control could arise when trolling a drop-off.

Consider your budget, too! Many used boats will work as well as many of the new models. They may only lack some of the more refined features like a false bottom floor to make walking or standing in the boat easier. To install this feature all that is needed is some 3/4 inch exterior plywood cut to fit the bottom contours of the hull. Live wells can be installed in any boat by using an old ice chest. Electric motors, anchor winches, bilge pumps, extra lights and comfortable seats can be installed in any boat to make them more fishable!

The Ranger boats are referred to as the "Cadillac" of boats and for a very good reason, they are built with the highest standards in the industry. These fiberglass boats are well designed on the inside to make fishing and the fisherman comfortable. The Ranger 1600 series is one style of boat pike anglers should take a close look at. In the last few years, Ranger has developed a new hull design that performs in big waves like many large aluminum boats, but is known among the serious anglers as a boat that offers exceptional control at slower speeds. Perfect for two anglers casting or three trolling this smaller size sixteen foot boat can be fished in a wide variety of ways.

The Ranger 1600 series of boat is one of the more ideal fishing rigs for pike. Although there is really no perfect boat for all fishing situations, this fiberglass boat is extremely versatile.

Outboard Motors

Selecting the proper sized motor for any boat is not an easy task. It would be nice to get your fishing spots in a hurry, but once there, it would be nice to have a small motor to do all the trolling so no undo wear is put on the bigger outboards. There are three options anglers can choose from to solve their boat control problems.

First, smaller boats are much easier to control than bigger boats of over 16 feet. This makes it possible to use outboard motors up to 35 horse power for good top end speed, but yet are small enough to troll down without too much problem.

The second option would be the use of a second motor, either electric or gas to maneuver the larger boats once you have zipped to the hot spot at fifty miles an hour. Some weather conditions will make it nearly impossible to control these larger boats with the smaller motors, but this would be an effective method 85% of the time.

The last option commonly used when selecting an outboard is the Mariner or Mercury 50 horse power motors. These motors will work very well on the majority of 17 to 18 foot boats. The unique feature that sets these motors apart from the others is their four cylinders. Most outboards have two or three cylinders which demand a much higher cylinder pressure which can lead to the fouling of plugs and the inability to troll at very slow speeds. Although motors with larger cylinders may get the boat around faster on the top end, they are rough and hard to run for prolonged periods at slower speeds.

Motor Maintenance

The outboard motors of today are much better designed and are more powerful and gas efficient than the motors of twenty years ago. The proper maintenance of these newer outboards should include regular tune-ups by a factory trained expert. All boat owners should get into the habit of taking their outboards into the shop each fall to have an expert tune-up and ready the motor for winter. This is one good way of having an expert

Changing plugs along with other simple maintenance tasks is one way of getting better performance out of your motor as well as preventing the majority of on the water problems anglers may run into.

spot any major problems that may come up. By waiting until spring, you may find the motor buried with hundreds of others.

Regular maintenance you can do yourself can help avoid many of the more common breakdown problems. Spark plugs are often fouled from excessive trolling or just too much carbon build-up inside the cylinders over the course of the year. By simply replacing or cleaning the plugs at least once a year, a very noticeable improvement can be noticed with a better starting and running motor.

The gear grease in the lower unit near your propeller must be checked monthly. If you notice the lubricant getting milky, water is seeping into the gear case and this could be a sign of a major problem. This lower unit lubricant does wear out under heavy use and should be changed at least twice every season. The cost of lower unit lubricant is cheap when compared to the cost of a new lower unit!

The oil mixed with the tank of gas is critical to the performance of the motor. Use **ONLY** BIA certified oil. Many discount two cycle oils are available, but the end result may be costly repair bills. Whatever brand you end up buying, be sure to check the label for BIA certification!

Electric Trolling Motors

One of the nicest ways to make a fishing boat more fishable is to add an electric trolling motor. The advanced design of today's electronics provides for better performance and efficiency than their predecessors.

Similar to outboards, the electric motors are available in different power rates and a balanced match with your boat is important. Many manufactures provide recommendations in their literature for selecting the proper size motor. The main purpose of an electric motor is to help move the boat about at slow speeds when wind and current conditions are low. The boat's main gas engine should be brought into use when times are too difficult for the electric motor to handle.

Motor designs are getting more efficient every year. A twelve volt power system is all many anglers will ever need for most fishing boats. A specialized marine battery however, is very important for supplying enough power to last all day long. The 105 amp deep cycle batteries, which cost about $100 each, are designed for electric motors and use of a regular car type battery will offer only disappointment.

At least a ten amp. battery charger is recommended for giving the battery a full charge overnight. When selecting a battery charger, be sure to get one with an automatic step-down feature or timer built in so it does not boil the battery dry.

A bow mounted electric motor is a good choice if you plan on doing a lot of casting, but will not work too well for trolling as the back end of the boat can easily swing around and lines will end up under the boat. A transom mounted motor is the best way to go when slow trolling is to be done. A lightweight electric motor can be easily clamped to the back of the boat in a position that is comfortable to reach while fishing. The cost of a transom mounted model is considerably less than the bow mounted counterparts.

Bow mounted electric trolling motors are very popular with bass and muskie anglers who do a lot of casting. Foot control models make it possible to maneuver the boat while keeping your hands free to cast. While mounted on the bow, these motors are able to pull the boat at a surprising rate without a sound.

A new feature on electric trolling motors is the weedless prop. This unique design makes it possible to run an electric motor through thick weeds without clogging up.

CHAPTER TEN

Pike Fishing Tips

This chapter deals with a variety of topics which may help your fishing success at any time of year. Pike fishing for centuries has been one covered with wives tales and superstitions that add to the fun, but may offer some interesting possibilities in modern-day strategies.

Big Fish, Big Bait

One point to consider about the size of bait to use in relation to the size of your catch. Consider some research that shows adult pike prefer to feed on baitfish ten to twenty percent of

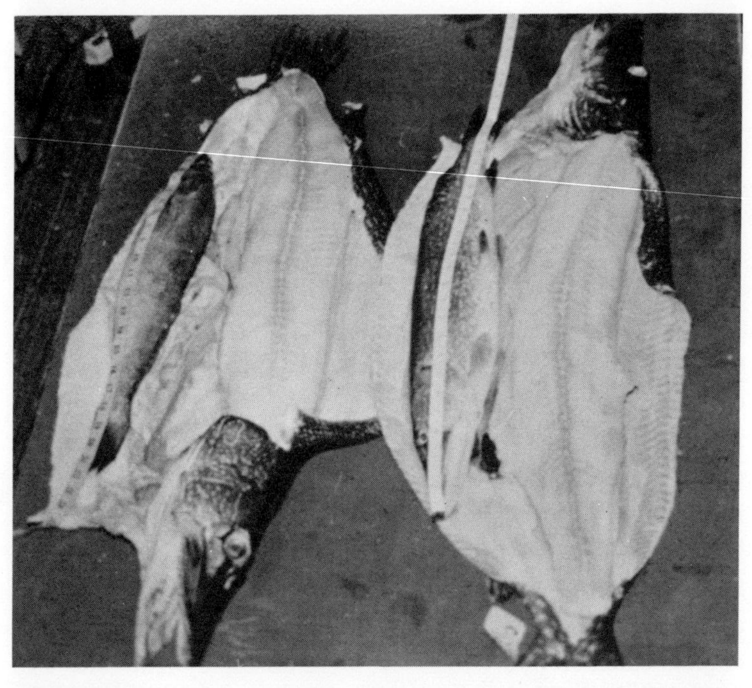

BIG EATERS! Al Landerville and Dave Cossak both from St. Paul, Minnesota took these beauties on large spoons from a lake in Saskatchewan, Canada. Al's 27 pounder had a 22" walleye in its stomach, and Dave's 24 pound pike had a 28" northern pike in it's stomach! In wilderness lakes where food is often scarce, bigger pike will feed on anything they can to survive. Photo by A-1 Taxidermy

their own body weight. If this is true, then to catch a twenty pound pike, an angler should use a minnow weighing two to four pounds! It has been well documented that pike have eaten other pike up to ten pounds. In the remote regions of Canada where there is a shortage of food, big pike are known to eat small beavers, muskrats and small ducks! One indian guide goes so far as to drag a walleye of about two pounds behind the boat on a stringer to get the attention of a big pike. When the fish attacks the bait he pulls the walleye away and drops a big spoon down behind the boat.

If it is true that larger pike prefer bait much bigger than what most anglers commonly use, what can fishermen do to make their baits look larger to the fish? One answer would be to use larger spinners and add extra bucktail or rubber to the hooks to help give the impression of a large bait without increasing the weight of the baits. The second would be the use of extremely large suckers, but anglers should be warned that unless the lake or river system has a high population of big pike, it may be a few years between strikes.

Selecting and Fishing a New Lake

To increase the chances of an angler catching a big pike, it pays to be on the right type of lake or river system. One of the cardinal rules in fishing for big pike is to fish a lake that has a lot of big pike in it in the first place! This, of course, is not an earth shattering fact, but what is important is to realize that many anglers spend all their time trying to catch one large pike that the Fish and Game people netted ten year ago. In this book there are over one hundred pictures of big pike taken by using a wide variety of techniques. The reason so many "expert" anglers catch so many big pike is because they fish lakes that have thousands of big pike in them!

Pike fishing for the big ones will involve the proper selection of a lake, along with the knowledge of the techniques we have already mentioned in earlier chapters. The biggest clue is when each lake is considered from a food fish standpoint. If a lake has the right type of forage fish, it can support a population of big northerns. This kind of information is kept on file for most major bodies of water in the fisheries office of the state or provincial Fish and Game Department in which the lake lies. By inspecting the abundance of ciscoes, whitefish,tullibee, smelt or trout, a lake may have can greatly increase the chances of pike growing to trophy size.

The time of year a lake is fished is also critical to the success an angler may have. Catching one big fish is, of course, pure luck in many cases. When anglers ask what time is the best time to be out fishing for big pike, the response is always "**ANYTIME.**" The suspense of not knowing when the trophy of a lifetime will hit can keep fishermen casting for days.

For the last few years one way of keeping in touch with the fishing grapevine is to subscribe to a weekly fishing magazine in your region. Up-to-date information is supplied to the papers, who strive to be as current as possible with activities in the fishing world. There has been more than one occasion when Jim Peterson's Outdoor News, a weekly fishing magazine published in Minneapolis, has put anglers onto some prime fishing waters when the fish were definitely biting. There are many such publications all across the country that can serve as a valuable source of up to date fishing information.

Record books also can serve as a valuable resource of big fish information. This is done by checking the results of any state or regional fishing contest. Many are sponsored by newspapers or sport shops with the results published weekly in the paper. By looking over the winners, it soon becomes apparent which lake or lakes have been producing the prize winning pike. This can be done on a weekly basis or on a seasonal basis with a special interest on the dates the fish were taken. Selecting a time for your annual summer vacation may in fact be a calculated process as to when the big pike in past years were caught.

Fishing buddies or sportsman's clubs can be a valuable resource of fishing information which can also save you time when you are out on the water. Getting a chance to talk with someone who has fished the lake, especially a good fisherman, can make for a dynamite trip. In any new lake situation there is always an adjustment period to decide which lures and places are holding fish. If someone has already done this task, more time can be spent catching fish. One word of caution, fish stories tend to dominate any conversation about a lake. Be sure to keep directing the questions to places and techniques instead of hearing about the big one that got away.

Fishing A New Lake

Every angler at one point or another comes face to face with one of the most challenging experiences in fishing, "how to find fish on a new lake."

The secret to success is taking time before the boat is launched to do a little research to gain a better understanding of the lake and area to be fished. Not only will this information be valuable for catching more pike, but it will also save a great deal of time knowing where the public access is, or knowing if many big pike even exist in the lake to begin with. All this plus much more can be learned even before leaving the house.

The first step in research involves getting a contour lake map to better understand how the lake is built. The Fish and Game Departments in most states have lake maps available, or they can be obtained through various sport shops who carry maps made by independent companies specifically for fishermen. Many of the small, lesser known lakes may be difficult to find, and only by contacting resorts or sport shops in the area can a map be found.

The second step involves getting background information about the lake. This is best done by making contact with the local Fish and Game Department to get the management history of the lake. The real secret here is making all that fancy biological information work to the fisherman's advantage, this can be done by having a better understanding of what certain facts mean and how it can affect your fishing success.

When calling for information about a specific lake, there is a wide variety of things that could be revealed about a lake once a little "reading between the lines" is done. Some of the major things to be aware of are listed below.

#1 Water Clarity
#2 Forage Fish
#3 Bottom Content
#4 Pike Density

Like piecing together parts of a puzzle, this information will give reliable information about the body of water to be fished. This biological information is not directly designed to help fishermen, so the terms may seem a little strange to the average angler.

The key to knowing how deep the weedline is knowing how far the sun penetrates into the water. Weeds can only grow as deep as the sun's rays permit, so a device called a Secchi disc is used to record water clarity. This disc is submerged into the lake and when it disappears, it will be exactly half the distance the sun can penetrate into the water. A Secchi disc reading of five feet means the weeds probably grow to ten feet! This may prove helpful in the selection of lures used to troll or cast the edges of a weedline.

Knowing the type of forage fish available in a lake is similar to a sign reading "Big Pike Living Here." The presence of ciscoes, tullibee, whitefish, shad, herring or even trout means the lake is capable of raising a northern pike to trophy size proportions. This of course does not directly mean the big pike will attack a lure. It does mean that if the fish are biting, there is a good chance a big pike will be around.

Having an understanding of bottom content is important to familiarize the lake to others you may have fished. Although no two lakes are exactly the same in every respect, they often have some very similar traits which can greatly enhance the speed and confidence in which the lake is fished.

Finding out the density of the pike population can directly effect your odds of catching a large pike. Test nettings are done on most lakes to determine what management steps will be needed to insure good fishing for anglers. At this time, many lakes will be classified into any one of several different management categories like bass/panfish lakes or pike/panfish lakes depending on the findings in the test nets. It would be a dead give-a-way to expect poor fishing from a lake classified as a panfish lake. Perhaps in the future, northerns will be stocked in the lake to manage the over population of panfish and a great pike lake may suddenly blossom! This leads us to also checking the lake's stocking history to find out if pike have indeed been used to manage over populations of other fishes. Through the use of test nettings, it is possible to get a good breakdown of fish size and quantity to have a very good understanding of all fish populations in a lake.

With the additional background information and a map in hand, it is time to launch the boat. Do not be in too much of a hurry when it comes to wetting a line. Take a few minutes and go for a little boat ride. Look at the shoreline vegetation and

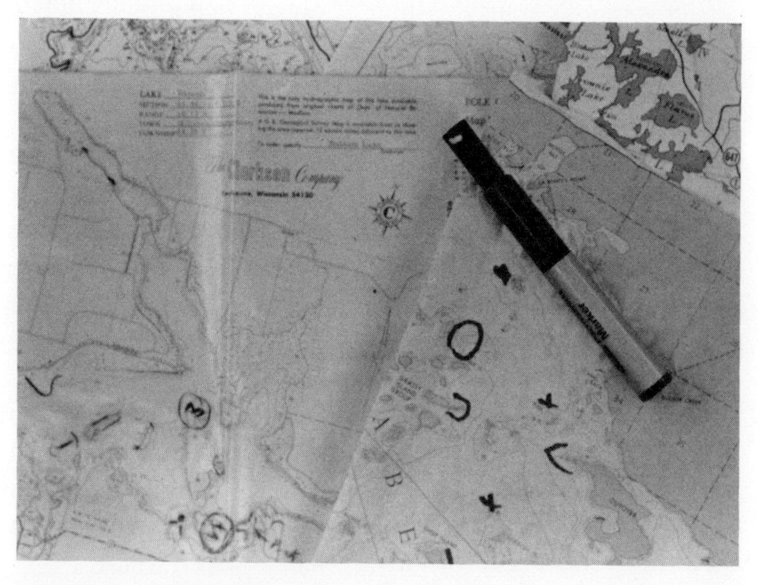

Lake maps aid the angler in many ways. Be sure to mark any "hot-spot" for future reference and record any special things that may be of interest on another trip.

how clear the water is. See if other pike anglers can be spotted and if so, what kind of areas are they fishing.

It is always a wise idea to start fishing any lake by fishing the unique contours of the lake bottom like points or sunken islands. One of the most underrated areas is the gap between land and an island. This area is called a saddle. If a narrow ridge of sand or rock is found in this gap, big pike love these areas. Do not waste time fishing every inch of a lake with hopes of running into a big fish somewhere along the line. Fish twenty yards either side of a point. If no fish can be found, move to the next spot. It is easy to get lazy and not be willing to move from one spot to another, but it must be done in order to find the fish.

Many of the best pike lakes are large and anglers are totally confused when they look at a maze of islands and bays. The real secret to catching fish on a large lake is to break the lake into small sections and instead of burning up six tanks of gas in a day, make it a point to fish only the areas close by. It is human nature to assume fishing is always better on the other side of the lake, but in truth, 99% of the time it is not.

The last thing to remember about fishing a new lake is to take the time and talk with other anglers you may meet. It may be a casual chat at the boat launch or a greeting as two parties come close together. Keeping the lines of communication open is one way of finding if the fish have been or are biting. Take note of the lures and methods the other boat is using and then decide if it is worth a try, or to continue fishing the way you have been. Keeping an open mind and being willing to adjust your fishing style is one sure sign of a good fisherman.

Sometimes no matter how hard you fish or what techniques are used the pike may not want to bite. It may seem there must be an answer to every fishing problem, but there is not. Once the new lake you are fishing has been fished thoroughly and not a single fish has been caught, then it is time to use a very reliable technique. It involves accepting the fact that on some days the big northern pike will not want to bite, so the frustrated angler is often well advised to leave the lake and head elsewhere! Even heading to a lake just across the road may be all it takes to cash in on some great pike action.

Shore Fishing Tactics

Many fishermen will not have access to a boat, and are limited to fishing from shore. Knowing how to select a good shore fishing area takes a little research. Follow the procedure we have already discussed about learning as much about the lake as possible. If any state agencies are contacted for information, take special note to where publicly owned land is located so anglers will not need to trespass on private property. With a lake map in hand, mark areas of deep water that look like they could be reached by casting from shore.

Shore fishermen are next advised to drive around the lake if possible and make note of any bridges or railroad crossings near the lake which may permit free access to the shore. These ares of improved shoreline are the most ideal situations a angler could ever hope to find. Take a look and see if any boulders have been stacked along the shore to keep it from eroding. This is often a sign that the shore has been dredged and the angler will have easy access to deeper waters.

Bridges crossing over rivers or creeks flowing into the lake are excellent places to fish from a boat or from shore with equal success.

Spinning tackle is recommended for shore anglers as it will give the greatest casting distances. Getting a long way from shore is not all that critical, but it gives the fisherman more flexibility with where the baits could be fished. Spinning tackle works with both bait fishing and artificial lure methods.

If a choice ever arises, anglers are advised to fish the wind blown shoreline. The pounding of waves against the shore attracts the baitfish pike like to feed on. It may be a hassle to fish an area with a twenty mile an hour wind blowing in your face, but it works!

Fishing from shore does not have to be an excuse for you not to go fishing. On every good pike lake, there is always a place to wet a line and get great results!

Wilderness Fishing Camps

Heading north to an isolated lake full of trophy-size pike is something every angler dreams about. This dreaming can be one of the major pitfalls of such fishing vacations. Just because the lake is in northern Canada does not automatically mean that big pike will be jumping all over the place. It never seems to fail that a fishing camp brochure is full of big pike taken from the lake, but actually they were taken twenty years ago when the camp first opened. It is extremely critical "would be" customers find out how many big fish were caught last year and when most of them were taken.

Sportshows offer a great chance to talk first hand with camp and lodge owners who are just waiting for someone to show some interest in a fish story or pictures which they hope will end up with a visit to the lake. This kind of first hand experience can work both ways for the fisherman who needs to ask the right kind of questions and not be lured into listening to some big fish stories.

Maybe one lake has been heard of before and the pictures look very impressive, so you approach a fishing camp to ask about accommodations. Ask to see a recent picture of the cabins, both inside and out. Ask for a listing of past customers so you can call to ask their opinion about the camp. Ask how many pike over fifteen pounds were taken last season and how many fishermen visited the camp last year as well. This will give you a better perspective on what your odds are of catching a nice pike.

Fishing trips to wilderness camps are not cheap, but if selected properly, they can prove to be a very rewarding and memorable experience. Do not be lured into a big fish story unless further checking proves the camp is located on a true northern pike mecca!

To catch trophy pike like this, anglers must choose the lake wisely. Not many lakes can produce 25 pound pike, taking the time to research each lake is the key to catching bigger pike this next season.

Northern Pike to be Mounted

Everyone hopes to catch a big pike, and when it finally happens, one of the best ways to remember the moment is to have the fish mounted. When a big pike is caught and the decision has been made to keep it for mounting, there are several things the angler should do.

Roger Tourville, an award winning taxidermist from A-1 Taxidermy in St. Paul, Minnesota, was quick to stress how critical the proper care of the fish can be in getting a good mount.

"We can only go so far to correct badly torn fins and mangled bodies," commented Roger. "The real secret to having a good mount is to have a good looking fish to start with. Many folks who catch a big fish like to drag it around. This can only cause undo damage to the fish and it just becomes harder for us to give them a good mount. That is why every customer who stops by our shop gets a checklist of things they should remember in handling a fish that is to be mounted."

1. Get fish wet
2. Smooth all fins down against body
3. A piece of cardboard may be folded and taped around tail
4. Wrap entire fish in a wet bath towel
5. Seal tightly in plastic bag
6. Wrap bag in newspaper
7. Freeze solid
8. Get to taxidermist as soon as possible

If the fish cannot be frozen right away, keep it is as cool as possible. One tip for anglers heading to the arctic in search of big pike would be to dig down to the permafrost frost layer in the ground and store your pike under ground until you are ready to head home.

NEVER try to gut the fish to be mounted, leave it whole! Another tip for anglers looking for a good mount is to pack along a jar of borax. When a trophy pike is caught, quickly club the fish on the skull to kill it. This method of clubbing a pike is highly recommended to avoid any unnecessary damage to the fins. Take the borax and rub it all over the pike's skin and be sure to rub it in to both sides of every fin. Let the fish simply dry for about an hour and then follow the wrapping and freezing procedures we have just mentioned. By rubbing in the borax as soon as the fish is caught it is possible to lock in the color patterns of the fish to help give the final product a more life-like appearance.

One tip to help select the taxidermist that will mount your trophy of a lifetime is take a look at other pike that have been done. If you like the way one of his previous mounts were done, stress the importance of trying to make your fish look like it. Too many times fishermen are disappointed with the final results because they simply dropped off or sent the fish in by mail with no further directions. What they thought they would get back and what they actually received were very different.

The cost to mount a fish is often in direct proportion to the experience and quality of the taxidermist. It is common to pay from $2 to $4 per inch for the mounting of a pike. It pays to shop around and see what kind of workmanship you like best in the taxidermists close to your home.

CHAPTER ELEVEN

De-boning Methods for Northern Pike

There is no disputing the fact that the northern pike is an outstanding sportfish. They are great eating too, but a fillet from a northern pike is a little different than that of other fish because they have an extra row of fine bones in their backs called "Y" bones. These bones can be a problem when eating. It is unfortunate that the proper information is not easily available to anglers wishing to learn the various methods to simply and effectively de-bone pike.The two methods shown in this book are actually simple when practiced a few times on larger pike. The fine bones of a fish under four pounds could make it very difficult to learn any of the de-boning methods at first. Larger fish have thicker bones which are much easier to see and feel as the fillet is cut.

De-boning a pike is not hard, it is often just one or two more steps in the fish filleting procedure which as many already know is best mastered with practice. It may be comforting to know there is no method of de-boning a pike that does not waste a portion of the fillet. It is not practical to get the job done without losing a small portion of the fillet.

Another problem anglers face is the bad smell of pike slim while cleaning the pike, and afterwards when the smell is on their hands. Salt will work very nicely for taking away the smell. Just wash with a liberal amount of salt and freshwater and slime smell will be gone.

Take this book right out to the fish cleaning shack and have someone read the instructions for each method until you find one which seems easiest. Practice makes perfect, take your time and see how easy de-boning a northern pike can be.

The simplest method found for de-boning northern pike begins by cutting in behind the gill plate down to the main backbone of the pike and along its side almost all the way to the tail.

To this point, de-boning a northern pike is the same as filleting a walleye. Note: It is important to keep the fillet attached to the main body of the pike for greater ease of handling later.

Once the first cut has been made, it is now possible to see the small white ends of those pesty "Y" bones we want to remove. Sometimes it pays to rub your knife over the fillet a few times to make the bone ends more visible.

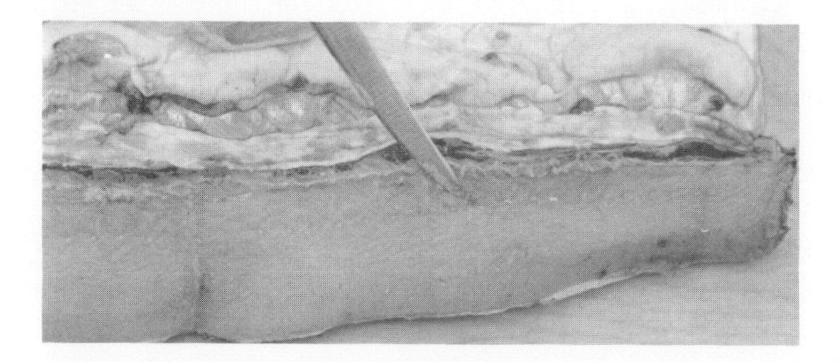

The first tricky cut is made along the top side of the "Y" bone ends working the knife down and along the bones. The bones will end just as the tail section of the pike begins. (There are NO "Y" bones in the tail meat of a pike.) Work along the one side of the "Y" bones until the outer skin is reached.

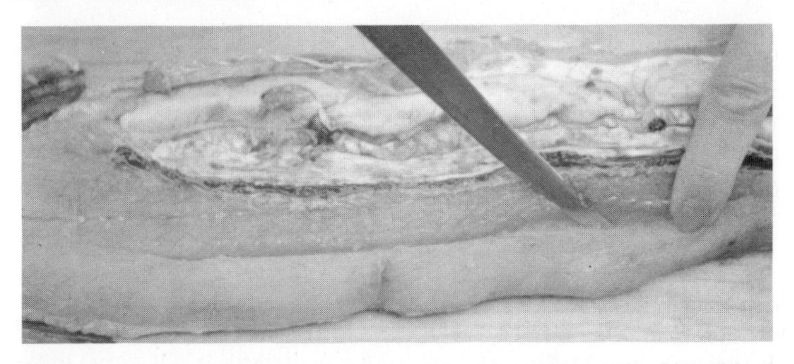

The same process begins now on the other side of the "Y" bones. Follow the bones by looking at the angle used in the first cut to accurately follow the bone line. Continue to follow the bones into the fillet until the skin is reached again. The bones will become thinner and thinner the closer you get to the outer skin.

Once the second cut is complete, the row of "Y" bones can be pulled out of the back fillet as shown.

With the "Y" bones removed, now it is time to remove the rib bones. This is done by having the tip of the knife follow under the rib bones with a series of short cuts as the bones are lifted.

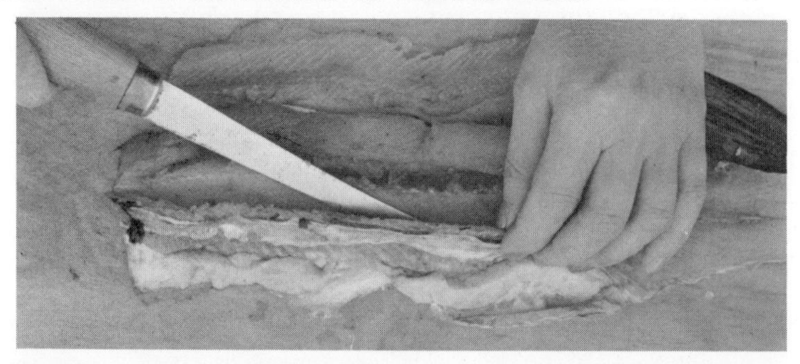

With the rib bones and "Y" bones removed, it is now time to remove the outer skin. This is the reason the tail is still attached to the skin, so it is easy to grasp. Hold the knife at a downward angle while the skin is pulled back and forth.

The finished side of de-boning a northern pike will look like this. If a great amount of red meat is found just under the skin on your finished fillet, anglers should scrape it away. This thin layer of red meat gives the fish a very undesirable flavor.

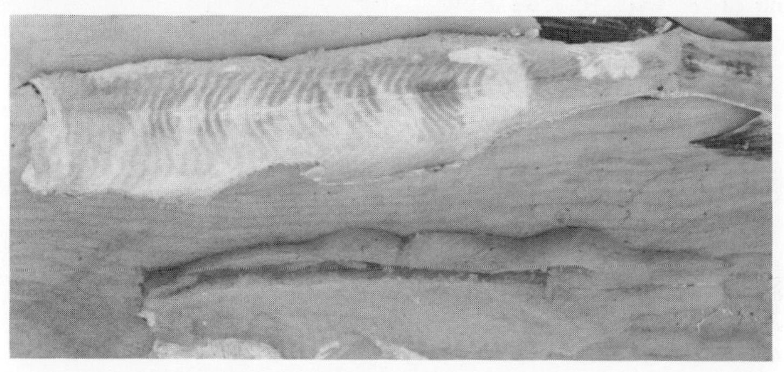

Another method for de-boning a pike may waste a little more of the fillet than the first method, but with practice this method can be used with great results. The first cut is made while the pike is laying on its stomach. The knife cuts down to the main spine and follows along its length until the dorsal fin is reached. This back section is often discarded on smaller fish, but on larger pike, it is possible to cut along the visual bone endings to remove all bones and skin.

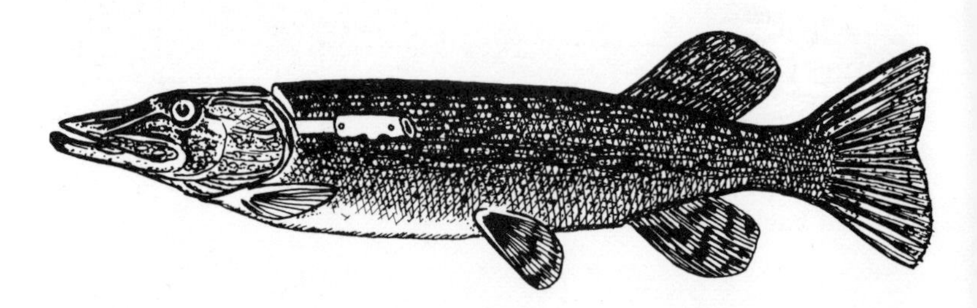

With the back section removed, the next cut is made while the pike is on its side to cut the fillet from the bone free tail section. The skin can also be removed during this step.

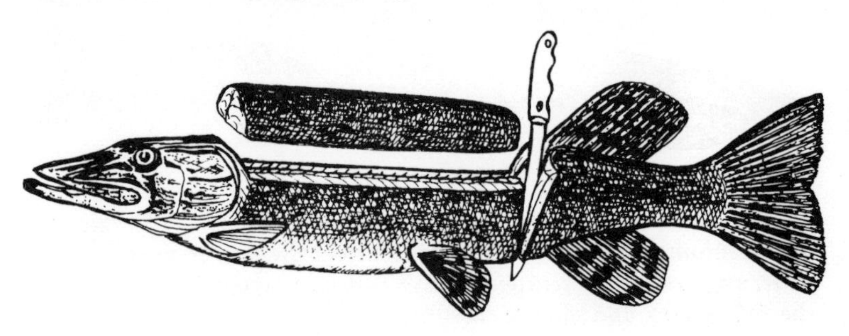

Putting the pike back on its stomach again, it is now possible to look down at the top of the rib section and cut downward along the ribs to remove the side fillet. Remove skin from this fillet as well, but first cut off all fins connected to the outer skin on the lower belly section.

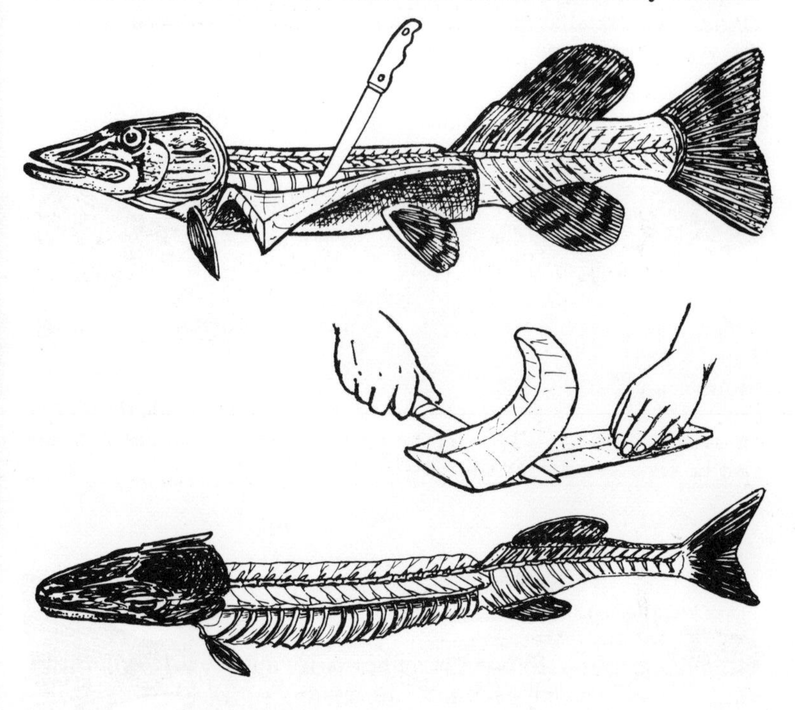

Great Pike Recipes

With Special Thanks to Margaret and Don Zenanko

Northwoods Pike Soup

3 lbs. Northern Pike fillets
1 quart water
Boil for 10 minutes. Drain and remove obvious bones.
1 quart of fresh water
Add: 1½ cups of fine diced potatoes
3 sticks of sliced celery
1 sliced carrot
1 heaping tsp. allspice
1 tsp. salt with a dash of pepper
When vegetables are tender, add fish and 2 large cans of condensed milk.
Simmer and serve.

Boiled Northern Pike

2 quarts of water
Add: 3 bay leaves
2 tsp. salt
¼ tsp. red pepper
Boil 10 minutes.
Drop fillets in and simmer 12 minutes. (Fish may be placed in cheese cloth bag or cooking parchment to retain shape.)
Serve with lemon juice and drawn butter.

Baking a Whole Northern Pike

Remove head, entrails and scales from pike.
Pour the juice of 2 lemons over fish.
Smother with at least one pint of sour cream.
Then cover with thin slices of lemons.
Bake 7 hours at 225 degrees. (Cooking times will vary with ovens, but the bones should be soft like canned salmon.)
Slice into small portions for serving.

Deep Fried Northern Pike

1½ to 2 lbs. de-boned pike fillets
Mix: 1 cup flour
    1 egg
    pinch of garlic salt
    1 cup of beer (room temperature)
Cut fillets into strips 1½ to 2 inches wide and place into batter.
Pour in 1 quart peanut oil and heat to 375 degrees.
Cook only 6 - 7 pieces at one time.
Cook until golden brown and floating on surface.
Season to taste.

Cooking a shore lunch adds a great new meaning to a day out on the water. Taking the time to enjoy the day and some freshly caught pike is all part of fishing.

Pickling Northern Pike

2 pounds pike fillets (de-boning completely is not necessary)
Cut fillets into 1 inch cubes.
Add: 1 cup pickling salt
6 cups water (this water must be pure)
Store in refrigerator overnight.
Drain brine solution and put fillets in white vinegar for another night.

Pickling Solution

½ cup granulated or brown sugar
½ cup distilled water
1 cup white vinegar
2 tablespoons pickling spices
3 to 6 cloves

Add cubed fillets, mix and bring to boil.
Simmer 10 - 15 minutes.
Pour into jars and seal.
Store in refrigerator for one week and shake jar once or twice while being refrigerated.
Store and serve when needed.

Special Pan Fried Northern

Soak fillets in milk for at least 15 minutes.
Prepare 3 bowls for dipping and a pan with peanut oil about 1 inch deep and heat to 375 degrees.
Cut the fillets into one to two inch strips.
First dip fish in bowl with flour.
Then dip into bowl of beaten eggs.
Then into bowl filled with potato buds.
Fry about 5 minutes on each side or until they are golden brown and the fish flakes easily.

Drawn Butter

Drawn butter is prepared by melting butter in double boiler over water. This gives the butter a very special flavor.

Tartar Sauce

½ cup mayonnaise
1 tablespoon sweet pickle relish
1 tablespoon minced onion (not grated or squeezed)
Dash of white pepper
Mix.

STATE RECORDS OF NORTHERN PIKE

State	Weight (Pounds - Ounces)	Angler	Location	Year
Alaska	38-0	Rhonda Edward	Fish Creek	1978
Arizona	24-3	Adolph W. Zeugner Sr.	Lake Mary	1981
Arkansas	16-1	Dick Cooley	Lake DeGray	1983
Colorado	30-1	Earl Walden	Vallecito Reservoir	1971
Connecticut	29-0	Joseph Nett	Lake Lillinonah	1980
Georgia	18-2	Keith Gragg	Lake Radun	1982
Idaho	27-5	D. Stuart Rude	Cave Lake	1982
Illinois	22-12	Robert Trusz	Lake Marie	1976
Indiana	26-8	Wayne Lewis	—	1972
Iowa	25-5	Allen Forsberg	West Okoboji	1977
Kansas	24-12	H. A. Bowman	Council Grove Res.	1971
Kentucky	9-8	Howard F. Renfo	Strip Mine Lake	1981
Maryland	20-13	Gary Peters	Patuxent River	1982
Massachusetts	29-3	—	Onota Lake	1979
Michigan	39-0	Larry Clough	Dodge Lake	1961
Minnesota	45-12	J. V. Schanken	Basswood Lake	1929
Missouri	18-9	Gene Moore	Stockton Lake	1975
Montana	37-8	Lance Moyler	Tongue River Res.	1972
Nebraska	29-3	Robert Philbrick	Sherman Reservoir	1976

Nevada	27-0	Kelly Maloperdos	Comins Lake	1978
New Hampshire	20-9	Richard Ryder	Spofford Lake	1978
New Jersey	30-2	Herb Hepler	Spruce Run Res.	1977
New Mexico	36-0	Paul Casias	Springer Lake	1978
	36-0	Samuel W. Roy	Miami Lake	1974
New York	46-2	Peter Dubuc	Great Sacandaga Lake	1940
North Dakota	37-8	M. Slind	Lake Sakakawea	1968
Ohio	22-2	Michael R. Smith	Lake Four Seasons	1981
Oklahoma	36-8	Raymond Fernandez	Carl Etling	1976
Pennsylvania	33-8	Gerald Enderle	Kinzua Lake	1980
Rhode Island	24-12	George Ray	Worden Pond	1980
South Dakota	35-0	Donald Matson	Lake Sharpe	1972
Tennessee	10-13	Charles Ed. Ankrom	Melton Hill Res.	1982
Texas	18-4½	Michael D. Sharpe	Town Lake	1981
Utah	19-2	Brent Newby	Raymond Lake	1982
Vermont	30-8	Bernard Golob	Glen Lake	1977
Virginia	22-9	Wm. R. Dobbs	Occoquan Res.	1976
Washington	18-6	—	Long Lake	1980
West Virginia	16-7	George Sasuccio	West Fork River	1982
Wisconsin	38-0	J. A. Rahn	Lake Puckaway	1952
Wyoming	22-8	Bryan Griffith	Keyhole Res.	1982
World Record:	55-15	Jiri Blaha	Lipno Res. Czechoslovakia	1979

NOTES